ASSISI AND THE RISE OF VERNACULAR ART

Frontispiece: San Francesco, View of Nave, Upper Church, Assisi

ASSISI
AND THE RISE OF
VERNACULAR ART

James H. Stubblebine

ICON EDITIONS

HARPER & ROW, PUBLISHERS, New York
Cambridge, Philadelphia, San Francisco, London
Mexico City, São Paulo, Singapore, Sydney

FIRST EDITION

Designer: C. Linda Dingler

Library of Congress Cataloging in Publication Data

Stubblebine, James H.
    Assisi and the rise of vernacular art.

    (Icon editions)
    Bibliography: p.
    Includes index.
    1. Mural painting and decoration, Gothic—Italy—Assisi. 2. Mural painting and decoration, Italian—Italy—Assisi. 3. Mural painting and decoration—Expertising. 4. Giotto, 1266-1337. 5. Francis, of Assisi, Saint, 1182-1226—Art. 6. San Francisco (Church : Assisi, Italy) I. Title.
    ND2757.A8S88 1985   751.7′3′0945651   84-43239
    ISBN 0-06-438556-6   85 86 87 88 89 MPC 10 9 8 7 6 5 4 3 2 1
    ISBN 0-06-430152-4 (pbk.) 85 86 87 88 89 MPC 10 9 8 7 6 5 4 3 2 1

Contents

v

Acknowledgments

Whereas a novelist or poet may work alone in a room, anyone who writes an art history book knows how much one reaches out for assistance: from associates, from students and colleagues in various countries. Many people offered me photographs, information, and ideas without which the project would long ago have foundered—everything I received was also an encouragement. Thus, I extend my thanks, first of all, to the Rutgers University Research Council for research monies, and to the College Art Association for travel funds that enabled me to sound out my thesis at the International Art History Congress in Vienna in September of 1983. I am grateful as well for support from the David A. and Leah Ray Werblin Foundation.

The assistance of Professor Hans Belting, the Dottoresse Ornella Francesci and Silvia Meloni, Padre Gerhard Ruf, Professors Barbara Lane and Anita Moskowitz, as well as Mr. Donald Beetham has assured that the book be as complete and thorough as I could have hoped to make it. To Lambertus van Zelst and Pamela England of the Museum of Fine Arts, Boston, and to Deborah Gribbon, former curator at the Gardner Museum, I extend my thanks for their help on the Riminese altarpiece at the Gardner.

My students also contributed in many ways, largely in the area of their fresh and always stimulating ideas. I should mention, among them, Kavin Frederick, Janet Zapata, John Lupia, Kristen Van Ausdall, and Stephan Wolohojian. Special thanks are due Mr. Wolohojian, who checked over the final manuscript, rescuing me from many a pitfall, and who contributed importantly to Chapter III.

The process of bringing the book into the light of day was a pleasant experience from first to last, for which the staff at Harper & Row deserve much credit. I thank particularly Pamela Jelley and the editor, Cass Canfield, Jr.

List of Illustrations

ASSISI AND THE RISE OF VERNACULAR ART

I

Introduction to the
Assisi St. Francis Cycle

In the whole range of Italian painting, few narratives of the life of a saint sparkle as do the murals of St. Francis' Legend in the basilica at Assisi (Frontispiece). It was no small artistic gift that visualized the chief events of St. Francis' life in such a way as to enrapture countless generations of visitors to the shrine. A 1920s guide, one of those little books written expressly for visitors to Assisi but of no scholarly consequence, is a typical example: the author was exhilarated by the narrative as people must have been the day of its unveiling.[1] An American Franciscan friar, who apparently played docent for English-speaking tourists, he echoed the sorts of things he daily told his clustered followers. And in scene after scene, he was swept away. When the young Francis renounces all his worldly possessions, Newton found the "superb palaces with their gay and pink tints worthy of our admiration." In the *Christmas Crib at Greccio,* scene XIII (Fig. 13), he exclaimed over the "various and picturesque costumes of the assisting faithful." When St. Francis appears to the Woman of Benevento, the author saw "terror and surprise in the features of the onlookers."

In other words, someone of our own era took the narratives at their face value. And anyone who has observed the enthralled tourists and pilgrims in the church of San Francesco today knows how true this is—the magic is still working. For them, as for our Franciscan friar, it is a narrative by turns gripping or charming but always true to life. The scenes have an immediacy that magnifies inversely to the untutored state of the viewer. It is this aspect of the series of frescoes at Assisi—that is, the phenomenon of popular or vernacular art—that we want to investigate.

The principal obstructions in such a study, however, are, first of all, the fame of the frescoes, which are as well known as any in all of Italian painting; and secondly, the immensity of the literature on the subject. Their very fame has, in a sense, been their undoing: everyone has had an opinion about them. Amid the superfluity of articles and books on the subject, the pictures themselves have sometimes been nearly forgotten. In a way, the fact that the frescoes were conceived during the same general time span when Giotto had his career has had an unfortunate effect on the history of art. From the first moment someone thought to attribute these frescoes to Giotto, it was never again possible to look at them without the cloud of Giotto hanging over and obscuring them. The defense of the Giotto authorship has often been put on an emotional level. Thus the nineteenth-century Italian critic Camillo Laderchi could say, "I would feel an invincible repugnance if I were to deny Giotto's authorship. . . ."[2] And Pietro Toesca, whose monumental *Storia dell'arte italiana* might presuppose a certain calm, wrote with considerable asperity of those who would deny the Assisi frescoes to Giotto, even, in the process, failing to notice that some of his arguments played into "enemy" hands.[3]

We should make it clear at once that the question of Giotto's authorship of the Assisi frescoes is not a central theme here. Rather than go over the endlessly repeated litanies of why Giotto was or was not the master of the St. Francis cycle, we expect the accumulation of evidence will assign the paintings their time and place in Italian art. The superficial resemblance in the Assisi cycle to Giotto's concepts of form is not much greater than in the work of a number of contemporaries, inevitably so, given the overwhelming impact of Giotto's innovations. Understanding this, we will, as we proceed, appreciate the way the Assisi painter or painters borrowed from Giotto: the utter differences from him will be revealed precisely in the nature of their adaptations. In the end, it will become increasingly apparent just how irrelevant such an attribution is.

One can understand how the stance against Giotto's authorship taken by Friedrich Rintelen in 1911 acted like an earthquake whose tremors and aftershocks reverberated for a number of years.[4] It is true that a number of critics, especially from Germany and Austria, followed his lead—Hausenstein, Rosenthal, and Schmarsow among them.[5] But for the most part the reaction was unfavorable. In Beda Kleinschmidt's monumental three-volume study of the basilica at Assisi, done in the 1920s, the author fulminated against Rintelen and would have had us believe his theories came to nothing.[6] More and more, Rintelen was held up as an extremist, as too unbending and idealistic. The reasoned study by Richard Offner, "Giotto, Non-Giotto,"[7] perhaps the quintessential Rintelenian statement, ultimately failed to persuade many critics, even those who recognized Offner's unusual visual acuity. Gradually, there has come into being a general consensus that Giotto's was the mind behind the series but that he was helped to a greater or lesser degree by one or a number of assistants. This has proved to be a more acceptable position for the majority of art historians insofar as the individual could decide for himself the degree to which he thought Giotto had been assisted, without running athwart the broad consensus which saw the St. Francis Legend as being in fundamental ways a Giottesque work.

On the other hand, the passion with which Giotto's involvement is defended should say something to us, if only because the arguments are indeed so often passionate and defensive. That is to say, one reads Toesca on the subject with the feeling that he has lost the battle without admitting it. He and others have always felt constrained to accumulate inordinate amounts of "evidence" to defend Giotto's authorship. Many a writer seems to have been led away from the truth because he discussed the Legend not in terms of what he saw before him on the wall but in terms of the Giotto he carried in his mind.

The cycle at Assisi needs to be examined afresh in terms of what preceded and followed it in San Francesco, Assisi, and elsewhere, especially in Florence and in Rome. Too seldom have the frescoes been examined against a broad landscape of contemporary painting by which we would infer an expanded period from around 1290 to around 1350.[8] Likewise, the identification of the painters with either the Umbrian or the Roman schools has been little explored in recent years, with the notable exception of Smart. Although this cannot be a theme here, we believe continued study will reveal that the painters in the workshop responsible for the frescoes were Umbrians trained in Rome or, at the least, by Romans.

It is not the intention here to set the stage for the reader by a complete account of the narrative. Excellent introductions abound, starting with the modern, thoroughly scholarly volume by Alastair Smart. There, as in a number of other places, one can learn details of the twenty-eight narratives arranged around the walls of the upper church and their brief, accompanying quotations from the *Legenda major* by the brilliant mid-thirteenth-century General of the Order, St. Bonaventure, who decreed that his interpretation become the official account of the saint's life.[9] We must be satisfied with the briefest laying out of the scenes, sufficient only to focus our attention.

The narrative begins on a lyrical note with the theme of the cloak so important to St. Francis and his views. In the first scene (Fig. 1), a simple man —that is, a simpleton—sees in the young patrician Francis spiritual depths of which more worldly folk are as yet unaware. As Francis walks in the town square of Assisi with its Roman temple behind him, the man throws his cloak to the ground for Francis to tread upon. And in the next scene (Fig. 2), it is Francis who compassionately throws off his own cloak to aid a needy knight. These are

1. (Top left) *St. Francis Honored by a Simple Man,* Scene I, Upper Church, Assisi

2. (Top right) *St. Francis Giving His Cloak to a Poor Knight,* Scene II, Upper Church, Assisi

3. (Bottom) *Vision of the Palace,* Scene III, Upper Church, Assisi

immediately perceived homilies—one a parallel to the honoring of Christ in the Entry into Jerusalem, the other a clear example of the noble charity so central to Francis' thought. In the portentous *Vision of the Palace,* scene III (Fig. 3), Francis sees the shields bearing the sign of the Cross which he and his knights (the Franciscan brothers) will bear on their mission.

The narrative continues through St. Francis' worldly acts, from the restoration of the little church of San Damiano just outside of Assisi that he was inspired to do while at prayer (Fig. 4). We are to understand that this act symbolizes the far larger task, to which he felt summoned, of restoring the Catholic faith. And, indeed, this is the substance of the dream-vision of Pope Innocent III in scene VI (Fig. 6). Between these two scenes is Francis' *Renunciation of Worldly Goods,* scene V (Fig. 5), a moment that heralds his new life and the beginning of the Franciscan Order—to which the pope gives approbation in the next group of episodes, scene VII (Fig. 7). Two highly symbolic scenes follow: the brothers' *Vision of the Fiery Chariot,* scene VIII (Fig. 8), in which the saint's role as the new Elijah is impressed on us, and the *Vision of the Thrones,* scene IX (Fig. 9), in which Francis sees that the most glorious of these is reserved for himself.

4. *Miracle of the Crucifix,* Scene IV, Upper Church, Assisi

5. *Renunciation of Worldly Goods,* Scene V, Upper Church, Assisi

6. *Dream of Innocent III,* Scene VI, Upper Church, Assisi

7. *Pope Innocent III Sanctioning the Rule,* Scene VII, Upper Church, Assisi

8. *Vision of the Fiery Chariot,* Scene VIII, Upper Church, Assisi

9. *Vision of the Thrones,* Scene IX, Upper Church, Assisi

In more worldly ways that folk can be sensible to, St. Francis causes the demons to be driven from Arezzo, scene X (Fig. 10), and he prepares to walk through fire in return for the sultan's conversion, scene XI (Fig. 11). Again, in a remarkably symbolic episode, we grasp that the *Ecstasy of St. Francis,* scene XII (Fig. 12), clearly parallels the Transfiguration of Christ. The north wall ends with the dazzling tumult of St. Francis inducing a vision of the Christ Child at a Christmas Mass in Greccio, scene XIII (Fig. 13). When we turn to the entrance wall, the *Miracle of the Spring* (Fig. 14) awaits us, like an idyllic climax to the first half of the drama, followed just across the main doorway by its twin, in which St. Francis preaches to the birds, scene XV (Fig. 15).

The left, or south, wall of the nave begins with the story of the death of the Knight of Celano, scene XVI (Fig. 16), after St. Francis had prayed for the man's salvation. The following episode of St. Francis preaching before Honorius III, scene XVII (Fig. 17), alludes to the fact that it was on this occasion

10. *Exorcism of the Demons at Arezzo,* Scene X, Upper Church, Assisi

11. *St. Francis Before the Sultan,* Scene XI, Upper Church, Assisi

12. *Ecstasy of St. Francis,* Scene XII, Upper Church, Assisi

13. *Christmas Crib at Greccio,* Scene XIII, Upper Church, Assisi

14. *Miracle of the Spring,* Scene XIV, Upper Church, Assisi

15. *Sermon to the Birds,* Scene XV, Upper Church, Assisi

16. *Death of the Knight of Celano,* Scene XVI, Upper Church, Assisi

17. *St. Francis Preaching Before Honorius III,* Scene XVII, Upper Church, Assisi

that the pope officially confirmed the Franciscan Rule. With this, we move toward the more exalted aspects of the end of St. Francis' life. In scene XVIII (Fig. 18), while St. Anthony of Padua is preaching to the Franciscan brothers at Arles, one of them has a vision of St. Francis appearing before the group. This prepares us for the even more other-worldly episode that follows, the *Stigmatization of St. Francis,* scene XIX (Fig. 19), by far the most famous element of St. Francis' Legend, in which the marks of Christ's wounds were impressed upon the body of the saint. It was the culmination of a life in imitation of Christ—a key aspect of Franciscan thought. After this we witness St. Francis' death and ascension into Heaven, scene XX (Fig. 20), the latter event witnessed by Brother Agostino and, in a dream-vision, by the bishop of Assisi, scene XXI (Fig. 21).

The *Funeral of St. Francis* might more properly be called a Verification of the Stigmata, scene XXII (Fig. 22), which parallels the Christological event of St. Thomas' verification of Christ's wounds. The story moves forward to the procession in which St. Francis' body is carried to burial, scene XXIII (Fig. 23), pausing at San Damiano where the Poor Clares were installed and where their founder, St. Clare, bends over the figure of St. Francis as though she were the Virgin Mary bending over the dead Christ in a Lamentation. The badly effaced

9

18. *Apparition at Arles,* Scene XVIII, Upper Church, Assisi

19. *Stigmatization of St. Francis,* Scene XIX, Upper Church, Assisi

20. *Death and Ascension of St. Francis,* Scene XX, Upper Church, Assisi

21. *St. Francis Appearing to Brother Agostino and the Bishop of Assisi,* Scene XXI, Upper Church, Assisi

22. *Verification of the Stigmata,* Scene XXII, Upper Church, Assisi

23. *St. Francis Mourned by the Poor Clares,* Scene XXIII, Upper Church, Assisi

24. *Canonization of St. Francis,* Scene XXIV, Upper Church, Assisi

25. *St. Francis' Apparition to Gregory IX,* Scene XXV, Upper Church, Assisi

26. (Top left) *St. Francis Healing the Knight of Ilerda,* Scene XXVI, Upper Church, Assisi

27. (Top right) *Confession of the Woman of Benevento,* Scene XXVII, Upper Church, Assisi

28. (Bottom) *Liberation of Peter of Alifia,* Scene XXVIII, Upper Church, Assisi

and undistinguished *Canonization,* scene XXIV (Fig. 24), follows. Then, in the last phase of the story, come the apparitions of the dead saint, when he appears to Pope Gregory IX, scene XXV (Fig. 25), to the wounded man of Ilerda, scene XXVI (Fig. 26), to the repentant woman of Benevento, scene XXVII (Fig. 27), and finally to the repentant heretic, Peter of Alifia, whom St. Francis liberates from prison, scene XXVIII (Fig. 28).

Smart has divided the narrative into seven "cantos": the prelude to his ministry; St. Francis revealed as savior of the Church; the prophecy of St. Francis' glory and of the reward for his humility; his ministry sealed by the stigmatization; his death and ascension; his funeral and canonization; and his posthumous miracles.[10] Even without the explanatory inscriptions that accompany the scenes, the thread of this narrative is never lost, but holds the viewer enthralled from first to last.

Although elements of the narrative will again and again preoccupy us, it is not the story itself that is our main interest; here, we have different concerns on which to concentrate. For one thing, the St. Francis cycle at Assisi will be examined in terms of another, though briefer, cycle of the saint's life in the Bardi Chapel of Santa Croce, as well as Giotto's other late frescoes in the Peruzzi Chapel of the same church. Other cycles of the saint's life of both the thirteenth and fourteenth centuries have a good deal to tell us about our series of scenes in Assisi. The Legend must also be looked at in the context of the rest of the nave decoration in the upper church, especially the earlier Old and New Testament cycles.

Much can be gleaned, I believe, from a reexamination of the various written Legends of St. Francis that became widely known at intervals during the course of the thirteenth and fourteenth centuries. Thus, while St. Bonaventure's Legend remained official, other versions that came into view from time to time had, with the ineradicability of apocrypha, a strong hold on the popular imagination.

Historical considerations ought, one supposes, to weigh heavily in explaining the long, protracted, and often interrupted campaigns of decoration in San Francesco at Assisi. Anyone at all familiar with Franciscan history will know of the enflamed controversy over the Spirituals within the Order, whose call for a renewal of the poverty principle was becoming strident during the last decade of the thirteenth century. By that time, such defenders of the poverty principle as Peter John Olivi, Ubertino da Casale, Conrad of Offida, and others had preached and spread the doctrine of the Spirituals' views widely among French and Italian Franciscans. Not until the beginning of the third decade of the fourteenth century was anything like a peaceful state restored to the Order.[11] We must presume, however, that the Conventuals, that is, the Franciscans within the Order who took a stand in favor of discipline and against the anarchical tendencies of the Spirituals, kept the upper hand through this period. One thing is certain: if the papal bull *Exivi de paradiso* that Pope Clement V issued in 1312 was conciliatory, the 1323 bull *Cum inter nonnullos,* issued by the greatest enemy of Franciscan poverty, Pope John the XXII, unequivocally closed the issue once and for all.[12] Thus, the date of the painting of the Legend can hardly be determined by historical circumstances within the Franciscan Order. In a larger sense, the discovery of the Legend's date depends on our understanding of the vernacularism that appears in the art of the developing fourteenth century.

During the course of the search we are to undertake, we will appear to be cumbered by a seemingly endless baggage of facts, data, inscriptions, iconographic details, and, above all, innumerable crisscrossing opinions, and to be confronted with an unseemly number of pictures from a variety of painters and schools. All of which, hopefully, will in the end illumine our landscape of fourteenth-century painting as the Assisi cycle of paintings assumes its proper place.

NOTES

1. F. Newton, *St. Francis and His Basilica at Assisi,* Assisi, 1926.

2. C. Laderchi, "Giotto," *Nuova antologia,* VI, 1867, 52.

3. P. Toesca, *Giotto,* Turin, 1941, 40–44, 50, and especially 59.

4. F. Rintelen, *Giotto und die Giotto-Apokryphen,* Leipzig, 1912.

5. W. Hausenstein, *Giotto,* Berlin, 1923; E. Rosenthal, *Giotto in der mittelaltarlichen Geistesentwicklung,* Augsburg, 1924; A. Schmarsow, *Kompositionsgesetze der Franziskuslegende in der Oberkirche zu Assisi,* Leipzig, 1918. These and many other opinions on the Legend are assembled in a useful though pedantic chart by L. Martius, *Die Franziskuslegende in der Oberkirche zu S. Francesco zu Assisi,* Berlin, 1932.

6. B. Kleinschmidt, *Die Basilika San Francesco in Assisi,* 3 vols., Berlin, 1915–28, II.

7. R. Offner, "Giotto, Non-Giotto," *Burlington Magazine,* LXXIV, 1939, 259–68; LXXV, 1939, 96–113.

8. Exceptions are the volumes by A. Smart, *The Assisi Problem and the Art of Giotto,* Oxford, 1971, and by G. Previtali, *Giotto e la sua bottega,* Milan, 1967. In both, the authors saw a broader spectrum.

9. These quotations from Bonaventure (*Legendae duae,* Quaracchi, 1898, 1923) are republished by Smart, *Assisi Problem,* 263–93, with the author's English translations. More detailed iconographical studies on the St. Francis Legend abound, including C. Mitchell's study of the theological program of the cycle, "The Imagery of the Upper Church at Assisi," in *Giotto e il suo tempo, Atti del Congresso internazionale per la celebrazione del VII centenario della nascità di Giotto, 24 settembre–1 ottobre 1967, Assisi-Padova-Firenze,* Rome, 1971, 113–34. In an analysis of Giovanni Bellini's *St. Francis* in the Frick Collec-

tion, New York, J. V. Fleming's considerable insights into Franciscan iconography project very well onto the Legend at Assisi: *From Bonaventura to Bellini, an Essay in Franciscan Exegesis,* Princeton, 1982.

10. Smart, *Assisi Problem,* 19.

11. For introductions to the poverty question, see J. Moorman, *A History of the Franciscan Order from Its Origins to the Year 1517,* Oxford, 1968; M. D. Lambert, *Franciscan Poverty,* London, 1961; and A. Holl, *The Last Christian, a Biography of Francis of Assisi,* New York, 1980 (original German edition, *Der letzte Christ,* Stuttgart, 1979).

12. By stating that it was heretical to say Christ did not own anything, the ground disappeared from under the Spirituals, whose basic premise this had been, as it had been for St. Francis in his *Imitatio Christi.* Continued resistance after this point was outside the mainstream of Franciscanism, confined to reckless groups known as the Fraticelli.

II

The Relation of the Assisi Cycle to Giotto's Santa Croce Frescoes

Franciscanism was a formidable force in Dugento and Trecento Italian art. Uncounted artists occupied themselves in creating the saint's image and recounting his Legend from the 1230s and, in the case of St. Francis' portrait at Subiaco, even earlier. An important panel with a cycle of scenes from his life, that in Pescia signed Bonaventura Berlinghieri and dated 1235, probably served as a model for a number of such panels created through the century in various places. The two best-known fresco cycles of the saint's Legend are the frescoes by Giotto in the Bardi Chapel of Santa Croce in Florence and those in the nave of the upper church of St. Francis at Assisi.

Whereas everything about the Assisi cycle always has been and still is highly controversial, the Bardi Chapel frescoes (Figs. 29, 30, and 35–39) have seldom offered any problem of attribution. By wide accord they are given to Giotto, and considered one of his later works, although their date within his later period is disputed.[1] This accord is the more unusual for an unsigned, undocumented work. The Assisi cycle is equally unsigned and undocumented, which has encouraged critics through the years to formulate various hypotheses for the authorship and dating of this cycle. For many, Giotto's authorship of the Assisi frescoes is the foundation on which every argument about the cycle is based. To state it at its simplest, such critics see these as early works, predating the Arena Chapel frescoes in Padua by some years. Thus, the Assisi paintings are generally placed around 1295.[2] For those who do not believe Giotto was involved, the date given them tends to be a little later. In recent years, however, the latest assignable date has been the year 1307—the date inscribed on the Giuliano da Rimini altarpiece (Fig. 76) in the Gardner Museum, Boston. This date is not, however, trustworthy, as we shall demonstrate later on, and it should not therefore be restrictive for the time of the Assisi frescoes.

The cycles of St. Francis' life in Assisi and in the Bardi Chapel have often been compared to one another, although, I believe, on a superficial level. Given the remarkable similarities wherever the two series overlap and the near identity of a number of details, a much more detailed analysis of these correspondences —as well as of the differences—would be a matter of the utmost consequence.

The literature is not without some discussion of the two together. Many years ago, Beda Kleinschmidt in his monumental work on the Assisi basilica said that in the Bardi Chapel, Giotto improved (the author used the word *verbessert*) those compositions he had made a quarter of a century earlier in Assisi.[3] Adolfo Venturi also wrote of Giotto's "gran progresso" over his Assisi frescoes and demonstrated how he amplified the motifs of his earlier series.[4] When we read Raimond van Marle on the authorship of the Assisi frescoes, we find him reiterating over and over again the dubiety felt by many others ("the authorship of this cycle as a work of Giotto's is anything but certain and not even generally admitted," or, "I know that today many art critics doubt or tend to deny Giotto's authorship. . . .").[5] Whatever van Marle may have really thought, he went on to say that Giotto was well enough pleased with his Assisi works to repeat several details in his Santa Croce frescoes. Thus, the gesture of someone restraining St. Francis' father in the *Renunciation of Worldly Goods* (Fig. 32) so satisfied Giotto that he increased the number of restrainers to two in the Bardi Chapel (Fig. 33), and imbued the figure of the father with more violence. Like Kleinschmidt, van Marle saw these changes as improvements of the artist's own earlier effort. This is the same approach we find in the recent scholarly volume on the upper church by Hans Belting, although in this case, the comparison is between Assisi and Padua. At Padua, Belting said, Giotto made corrections *(Korrekturen)* of the Assisi compositions as well as improvements *(Fortschritte)* in interpretations.[6]

The notion of an artist correcting and improving his own earlier work is, of course, plausible, often inevitable. When Titian returned to a theme from decade to decade, he reconceived it ever anew. On the other hand, an original creation and a variant or imitation of it by another artist is an altogether different matter, involving an appreciation on our part of the artistic process itself. It is in such a light that the relationship between the Assisi St. Francis cycle and the one in Santa Croce should be analyzed.

One might begin with the *Apparition at Arles,* scene XVIII (Figs. 18 and 29). In both versions, St. Francis appears in the door of the chapter house at Arles, where a visitor, St. Anthony of Padua, standing on the left, delivers a sermon on the Cross and its superscription.[7] As so often in the Franciscan Legend at Assisi, a vision is had not by a principal protagonist but by someone else present on the occasion, in this case a monk named Monaldo. Monaldo saw St. Francis in the doorway levitated above the floor, his arms spread out like Christ's on the Cross. In the episode at Assisi, St. Francis simply stands there inside the room, his arms spread wide. In the Bardi Chapel, Giotto emphasized the apparitional by an ineffably refined posture he invented for the occasion: St. Francis is positioned neither inside nor outside the room; rather, he floats just in the central archway, arms raised to form a mandorla. Since he blends so completely into the compositional network, he is more easily perceived as dematerialized, with a consequent spiritualization of the figure. With Giotto, each monk sees St. Francis in the mind's eye; as Bonaventura expressed it, each knew "a consolation of the spirit."

In the Bardi Chapel version of the *Apparition at Arles* (Fig. 29), the composition is especially successful. The movement ripples from arch to arch, from column to column, establishing a strong surface design, together with an arrangement of architectural rectangles over the entire surface from the marble plaques in the foreground to the background panels. This surface design is

29. Giotto, *Apparition at Arles,* Bardi Chapel, Santa Croce, Florence

discreetly punctuated by quiet figures three layers deep. Every impulse to move into deeper space is countered by the strength of the rhythmic design across the surface. The composition is a triumph of mural decoration—the equal of what Raphael achieved in his *School of Athens*—and represents a stage in Giotto's thinking far more sophisticated than in the Arena Chapel frescoes.

At Assisi (Fig. 18), the apparition takes place inside a room instead of a cloistered courtyard. Unlike the effect on us of extraordinary simplicity in Giotto's setting, the room at Assisi is treated with elaborate cosmatesque decoration and double (trefoil) windows. Both the room and the benches on which some of the monks sit are canted on a diagonal as a means of emphasizing depth. St. Francis has thrown up his arms but now, at Assisi, his arms are well inside the room, not, as with Giotto, level with the door frame. Consequently, the saint seems to be physically present and without any supernatural flavor whatsoever. It is typical that the Assisi artist should adhere so literally to the story. There the narrative shifts from the visionary aspect to the concrete emphasis on the words of St. Anthony and the consequent vision in which Monaldo alone saw the saint in a cruciform posture. But we should remember that if the Assisi artist was adhering to the literal meaning of the episode, he did so as an alteration of a scheme originally devised earlier by Giotto in the Bardi Chapel.

The arrangement of the monks is different, too. Whereas Giotto makes us aware of the interior nature of the vision, especially through the downward glances of the friars seated toward the left, the Assisi version has them glancing alertly every which way. Most of them attend to the words of St. Anthony and do not notice St. Francis, except, of course, for Monaldo, who gazes concentratedly at the vision in the door. The difference speaks out: in the Bardi version, the focus of attention on a single spiritual experience is unmistakable; the fracturing of focus is a striking feature of the Assisi interpretation.

The comparisons continue: at Assisi, the monk seated on the ground in the center with his back to us and a sliver of profile turned to the right is almost identical to the figure under the left arch in the Bardi Chapel scene. Can we be asked to suppose that Giotto repeated one of his own figures so precisely a quarter of a century later? Or could we be looking at a "copy," made by a less capable artist a few years after Giotto's rendering in Santa Croce? The same is true of St. Anthony: as Previtali has pointed out, the two representations of the saint are in almost identical posture. Of course, for Previtali this measures the certainty of Giotto's authorship of both.[8] I believe, though, that it is just that near exactitude that bespeaks the hand and the mind of a copyist who has studied his prototype in the Bardi Chapel very carefully. The monks in the Assisi version are undeniably "Giottesque" in the bulkiness of their figures and in the fall and fold of drapery, yielding a clear line of the waist and bulky sleeves. The difference, amusingly enough, is that hardness of contour to the Assisi draperies that Toesca described so well and which he said was not found at Padua—thus unthinkingly undermining his own stoutly held belief in Giotto's authorship of the Assisi frescoes.[9]

As we have described the Giotto scene in the Bardi Chapel, it is a subtle balance between two- and three-dimensional space. His use of the serene court-yard of the chapter house as his setting may have been premised on its suitability for this spatial play between arches, columns, walls, benches, and every other architectural shape and object available to him. It was, then, perfectly logical for the Assisi artist to move the narrative to a more appropriate indoor setting, at the same time freeing the composition for greater play between the figures in what he might have considered a more interesting space. What he did, in effect, was to invert the architecture of the Bardi Chapel scene so that we are placed inside a three-dimensional room, looking toward the back wall whose windows open onto that courtyard which had been Giotto's setting. And we visually take in the careful detailing of the underside of that sloping roof so marvelously observed that it becomes part of the subject matter.

Only after perceiving this do we realize that the sloping roof in Giotto's scene had been more of a compositional shape, a part of a harmonious whole, than a physical property of a building, even though it satisfactorily performed that function. Oertel maintained just the reverse, that one had to know Assisi to understand a later Bardi version in which an artist (not Giotto, according to Oertel) contrived to make everything into a two-dimensional pattern. But when we try to apply Kleinschmidt's dictum that Giotto "improved" the picture in his later Bardi version, we have a difficult time of it. Looked at from the viewpoint of those who believe Giotto's Bardi Chapel scene follows later than the Assisi rendering, it would seem to be outside the parameters of Giotto's thinking for him to adapt the Assisi rendering to his own needs in Santa Croce—correcting the position of St. Francis, correcting the glances of the various monks, moving the setting to an exterior, and so forth. In each of these things, the Assisi picture has the look of an imitation, often ill-digested, and in many details graceless. But the Assisi version does express one typical concern of that series of frescoes: verism. That is to say, the sermon by St. Anthony *should* be depicted inside the chapter house, not in some outdoor setting, while Monaldo and no other should so consciously gaze directly at St. Francis. Even here we see that the Assisi artists looked to the realities rather than to generalities and the non-specific.

Another of the Bardi Chapel narratives that recurs in Assisi is the *Renunciation of Worldly Goods,* scene V (Fig. 5). Giotto's in the Bardi Chapel (Fig. 30) is extraordinary in the circularity of the composition—the curving movement of figures and architecture, swelling forward toward the center from recessive sides. Giotto relied heavily on the bold angle view of the large palace: the structure is astonishing in the way it exists as a compositional device, dividing and contrasting the two groups of protagonists. Francis, at a turning point in his life, stands partly around the corner from his father on the left. Thus the angle of the building is also a psychological borderline. In the Assisi rendering, it is quite otherwise. Although the episodes to either side of the scene (Fig. 31) are composed so as to lead our glances toward the center of the *Renunciation* and to emphasize the confrontation of forces, that center is relatively energyless. A chasm opens up between two clumps of buildings; they are two complexes that chatter and quarrel like magpies, distracting us from the business at hand. These little accretions of toy buildings are more of a diversion than anything else, with their staircases, fenestrations, angled roofs, and bright colors.

In Giotto's scene, it is a different sort of pleasure pondering that ingenious, spatially provocative loggia on the second story of the bishop's palace. The artist's evolution from the Arena Chapel series can in part be measured by such an achievement as this. While the architecture serves the story in an admirable way, it is just as important as an investigation of a structure with heavy masonry walls and with the virtuoso treatment of the open loggia above, including the judicious placement of its columns seen at various angles of vision. The blunt stoniness and cubic density of the lower story are the opposite of that open, airy, space-enclosing superstructure. Such an edifice has an intellectuality about it that probably impressed other artists such as, for instance, Donatello (the *Miracle of the Ass* relief in Padua). On the other hand, is it not likely that the Assisi artist —always more limited in his vistas, however active he was in the art of imitation —might have designed his little rooftop loggia on the right of his scene in response to Giotto's in the Bardi Chapel?

In both renditions, St. Francis, naked from the waist up, raises his hands skyward in a prayerful gesture. In both, the bishop of Assisi covers the boy with his cloak, turning his head away from the saint's nakedness (and, we may imagine, calling for an attendant to bring some clothing). If we were to take nothing but this group of St. Francis and the bishop, the evidence of a connection between the Bardi Chapel and the Assisi Legend would be inescapable. If we were to pursue such elusive matters as the way Giotto suggests, by the very drape of the bishop's robe, the bonding of the lad to the Church, or the subtleties of St. Francis'

30. Giotto, *Renunciation of Worldly Goods,* Bardi Chapel, Santa Croce, Florence

31. Scenes IV, V, and VI, Third Bay on Right, Upper Church, Assisi

pose in Giotto's rendering, we would begin to understand the Assisi group as an imitation of the Bardi original.

The father in Giotto's Santa Croce scene is a powerful image (Fig. 33): a massive figure, full of strength and determination, he leans forward as though to hurl himself at his son. The pose suggests the uttermost of fury and also of frustration at this son who is abandoning his family. It is at once a posture of rage, anxiety, and sorrow, which gives Giotto's rendering a special power and even poignancy. At the same time, the father, Pietro Bernardone, is pulled back so energetically by his companions that his torso is forced around to an almost full frontal view, creating a vigorous contrapposto. At Assisi (Fig. 32), the father does not lean forward but stands straight. His right arm is not pulled sharply back away from his body so that the gesture loses drama and even significance. The artist seems not to have been interested in or capable of the tension of Giotto's explosive figure, a figure that almost becomes the center of attention in the Bardi Chapel scene.

One detail of the *Renunciation* at Assisi puzzles us. The two children at the left (Fig. 32) appear to be caught up in the excitement of the event, pointing and talking together. Contrariwise, Giotto in the Bardi Chapel clearly illustrates another facet of the story: as St. Francis was hauled through the streets to the cathedral, the people, thinking him mad, shouted insults at him and children threw stones. At either side of the Bardi Chapel scene, a child with a skirt full of stones is restrained by an adult. No doubt desirous of evading the issue—probably thinking it unseemly to show such an incident about St. Francis—the Assisi artist borrowed what may have been a well-known grouping, the two children on the left of Giotto's *Flight into Egypt* (Fig. 34) from the Arena Chapel in Padua. The left of the two is in profile, leaning forward slightly, right arm extended, left hand holding a loop of drapery, while the other figure turns to regard him. One is reminded of the article in which Roy Fisher pointed out that the boy in the tree in *St. Francis Mourned by the Poor Clares* (Fig. 23) must have had as its prototype the *Entry into Jerusalem* in the Arena Chapel, where this motif belongs iconographically.[10] One inclines to the notion that the Assisi artists had drawings of various works to guide them, including details of the Arena Chapel frescoes. In any case, the ingenious symmetry of Giotto's two figures in the Bardi Chapel scene—fit to close the ends of a classical pediment—must have eluded the Assisi artist.

Nowhere in Giotto is there a more aggressively defined interior space than in the papal room used for the Bardi Chapel scene, *Honorius III Approving the Franciscan Rule* (Fig. 35); as a fully three-dimensional interior, it registers an

32. (Top) Detail of Fig. 5

33. (Bottom) Detail of Fig. 30

advance from such a scene in the Arena Chapel as the *Christ Before Caiaphas,* where he had also created such an interior. In a sense, the greater satisfaction we derive from the Bardi Chapel scene is due to the geometrization of the composition: the modulations of the back wall and ceiling in regular rectangles, the echo of the gables in the half gables, the gentle governance of the architecture over the figures so that, for example, those in the lateral spaces just fit the area to which they are consigned. Again, as in the *Apparition at Arles* (Fig. 29), Giotto heightens the tension between the two-dimensional and the three-dimensional elements, always allowing the two-dimensional that slender advantage suitable to mural decoration.

At Assisi, the much fuller cycle includes an earlier episode of 1309, in which Pope Innocent III had sanctioned St. Francis' Rule (Fig. 7), which was only finally confirmed by Honorius III in 1223.[11] Incontestably, scene VII at Assisi resembles the Santa Croce composition (Fig. 35), if only in the grouping of the Franciscans in several layers behind St. Francis and the raised position of the pope flanked by two cardinals. The architectural setting is, however, of a different sort altogether. Nevertheless, it is a remarkably aggressive statement, using such familiar elements as cosmatique work and elaborate brocaded hangings. The sculpturesque brackets uphold a series of small barrel vaults whose depth is described by (now almost vanished) coffers. More than almost any other scene in the cycle at Assisi, the setting overwhelms the narrative, which can only be arrived at if one searches beyond the obstacle of this setting.

Another episode from the Legend of St. Francis occurs in both the Bardi Chapel and the upper church at Assisi, *St. Francis Before the Sultan,* scene XI (Figs. 36 and 11). At first glance, the two renderings appear not to have much in common. In part, this is because the hesitant Assisi Master clings to the older Cavallini notion of the structure seen from an angle, as in several instances from St. Paul's outside the Walls such as the niche in the *Massacre of the Egyptian Firstborn* (Fig. 59),[12] and the mosaics at Santa Maria in Trastevere. Thus, the structure to the left topped by an open loggia and the throne-niche on the right are sharply canted inward toward one another in a disruptive, non-perspectival way that overwhelms the groups of figures by unduly drawing our attention from them. Giotto, on the other hand, has contrived a supremely simple, uncomplicated arrangement, involving a lively symmetry from side to side. The flat back wall rules the composition; a remarkably space-enclosing throne at the center contains the figure of the sultan of Babylon without very much disturbing the general shallowness of the space Giotto wanted to present. Likewise, the two side walls work very well to express the limits of the room without bearing down too much on our consciousness.

34. (Top) Giotto, *Flight into Egypt* (Detail), Arena Chapel, Padua

35. (Bottom) Giotto, *Honorius III Approving the Franciscan Rule,* Bardi Chapel, Santa Croce, Florence

36. Giotto, *St. Francis Before the Sultan,* Bardi Chapel, Santa Croce, Florence

It is here especially that we see the difference from the insistence of the architecture in the Assisi scene. At Assisi, St. Francis takes centerstage, but to no avail; we are drawn rather more to the imposingly enthroned sultan on the right and to the frightened heathen on the left. In a master stroke, Giotto in the Bardi Chapel scene places the sultan in the center: by glance to the heathen, by gesture to St. Francis, it is the sultan who unifies the elements of the story. For Giotto, the true counterpart to St. Francis is the figure in the great, splendid array of yellow drapery on the left who, raising some folds of the cloth as though to ward off this mysterious ritual of trial by fire, symbolizes heathenish non-believers. In the most marvelous way, the steep triangulations and peaks of his drapery echo the compositional lines of the sultan and of the flames.

The same figure on the left of the Assisi version is, as Smart said, the most expressive of the scene in its vigorous contrapposto.[13] But it is an ungainly figure, no doubt inspired by Giotto's; he fears only the flames, not, as in Giotto, the unknown and the awesome. At Assisi, this figure is in full flight glancing back over his shoulder. In Giotto's figure, the impulse to flee is checked, the figure seems to pause in flight and turn to look back. At Assisi, the artist has very much simplified the Giotto figure to a standard contrapposto one. According to van Marle, this Bardi Chapel episode "repeats many details" of the Assisi scene.[14] We would say, on the contrary, that the Assisi artist borrowed some of the elements from the Bardi Chapel but everywhere simplified the story to increase its impact. He also discarded what must have appeared to be an uninteresting, not very dynamic setting according to the different tenets of the Assisi masters.

In discussing the Santa Croce series vis-à-vis a supposed earlier date for the Assisi frescoes, one ought to examine the notion of "improvement" with the greatest care. When, for example, we read van Marle more closely, we discover him using such phrases as "simple repetition," "repeating many details," or "identical poses," as his means of assuring us and himself that Giotto painted both cycles. This would certainly be an uncomfortable concept of how Giotto worked; never do great masters resort to simple repetition or use identical poses, either from one work to the next or over a span of elapsed time. Furthermore, the notion that Giotto—whose inventiveness and imagination so marvelously opened to full bloom in the mature frescoes of the Bardi Chapel—would have proceeded in this fashion, is unacceptable.

Another of the scenes in the Bardi Chapel in Santa Croce that reappears in the Assisi series is the *Death and Ascension of St. Francis* (Figs. 37 and 20), a sequential arrangement of two such episodes that is usual and is found again, for example, in the Simone Martini Chapel in the lower church (Fig. 88). The similarities are to be understood only if we include in our analysis the Assisi *Verification of the Stigmata* (scene XXII). There are a number of correspondences. Of course, there are just so many ways to arrange a group of mourners around a deceased figure, but in both of these scenes three friars hold standards at the foot of the bier. Both have kneeling figures in the foreground, their backs to us. In both, one monk kisses St. Francis' foot while at his head another monk gazes sharply upward, his glance leading us to St. Francis' Ascension (a half-length figure framed in a mandorla held by angels).

In both, one or two citizens look on at the left. One difference is that no one kisses St. Francis' hand in the Assisi version; the artist included that motif in the *St. Francis Mourned by the Poor Clares* (scene XXIII). Likewise, the foreground figure, the Knight Jerome, inserting his fingers into the wound in Christ's side, is omitted at Assisi; or rather, it becomes the central theme of the *Verification of the Stigmata* (Fig. 22). The friar (Brother Leo?) seen just behind St. Francis'

37. Giotto, *Death and Ascension of St. Francis,* Bardi Chapel, Santa Croce, Florence

head glances and gestures upward dramatically toward the Ascension, guiding us to see it as well. This motif is included in the Assisi version too, although with less effect inasmuch as the figure who gazes up is amongst a throng around the saint's head.[15]

The *Death of St. Francis* (scene **XX**) in the upper church is the most populated episode in the cycle. Uncounted numbers of Franciscan friars and clergy fill the area from side to side, while angels—ten in number—swarm over the sky. Alas, the mass of figures behind the bier seem to be somewhat levitated and without a suitable sense of gravity. No doubt this was due to the artist's inability to convey the sense of the terrain at the scene of the saint's death down in the valley at a spot known as the Portiuncula. An unfortunate effect is that St. Francis' figure drops down to the bottom quarter of the scene. One cannot escape the feeling that the Assisi artist found the Giotto figures in the foreground of the *Apparition at Arles* (Fig. 29) more suitable sources for his own foreground mourners.

Once again, we must ask ourselves whether Giotto would have borrowed so many elements from what is one of the less distinguished narratives at Assisi

29

and created order out of its chaos, or whether it is not the other way around. Certain it is, the similarities are not happenchance. Certain it is, Giotto's power of concentrating his forces in a composition yields a mournful expressivity that sweeps through the attending figures. It would not be wrong to compare this scene with the famous *Lamentation* in the Arena Chapel for the intensity of the emotion shared by a good number of participants. It resembles the Padua scene also in the arrangement of the figures around the bier, creating overlapped layers of figures who themselves generate a depth of space in the pictorial field.

Above, in both the Bardi Chapel and the Assisi scenes, St. Francis appears in a mandorla in a conventional ascension arrangement. Giotto's figure is not only three-quarter length but seen from slightly to the left, and these features enhance the sense of swift movement upward, all of which contrasts with the figure at Assisi: bust-length, static, frontal, orant. This is, of course, a more satisfactory representation as far as the Franciscan Order might wish to have it seen. One curious detail demonstrates how the Assisi artist consistently sought this different effect. In the Assisi *Ascension,* the two lower angels are symmetrically disposed in profile, facing toward St. Francis, whereas the upper two are facing forward and glancing outward. In the Bardi Chapel *Ascension,* the two angels on the left are seen in profile, whereas the two on the right are seen full face. As a result of this combination, the sense of propulsion upward and toward the right side is more strongly felt. At Assisi, movement is halted by a determined symmetry. One suspects that the Assisi artist wished to play down the flourish of movement that electrifies the Giotto representation.

The necessity to condense the Legend of St. Francis to a few most characterizing and significant episodes is everywhere apparent at Santa Croce. One has already seen Giotto's genius for condensation and elision at work in the Arena Chapel in Padua. In the Bardi Chapel, the artist brought together the vision of *St. Francis Appearing to Brother Agostino and the Bishop of Assisi* (Fig. 38) by the device of separating the two episodes with a small, rectangular baldachin, which diverts our attention away from the fact that two widely separated rooms are being represented. At the left, Brother Agostino rises on his deathbed as he sees, in his last gasp, St. Francis ascending to Heaven. At the same moment, to the right, Giotto represented St. Francis appearing, during his ascent, to the sleeping bishop. By the emphasis on the reaction of the mourning monks around Agostino's bed, Giotto lessens the hieratic content of the scene.

This is in marked contrast to the Assisi rendering, scene XXI (Fig. 21), where, in any case, the scene containing the two episodes is dependent on and must be seen in conjunction with the preceding narrative, the *Death and Ascension of St. Francis,* scene XX (Fig. 20). Thus Brother Agostino, turned now to the left, raises his arms and cries out as he sees the ascendant St. Francis in the preceding narrative. It must be admitted that the Assisi artist succeeded well in enlivening his double scene (XXI) of the two visions, with spaces rendered by architectural recessions, along with rich furnishings and a variety of decorations. So austere a layout and so unostentatious a space-generating device as the baldachin in Giotto's bare scene would have no appeal in the Assisi scheme of things. When we study the way Giotto evinces so much spatial play with such spare means, we are entranced.

The *Stigmatization of St. Francis* (Fig. 39) is dramatically placed just outside and above the arched entrance to the Bardi Chapel, visible from a long ways off in the nave of Santa Croce. A comparison between this fresco and its counterpart in Assisi (Fig. 19) illuminates much about the relationship between the two cycles. In the Bardi Chapel, following the tradition, St. Francis kneels and gazes up to the Seraphic Christ, who implants the stigmata on his hands, feet, and chest. The site is a mountainous wilderness, occupied by a small chapel and behind the saint the aperture of a cave. The principal differences in the Assisi version are the addition of a seated brother absorbed in his book and, on the left, a second chapel in lieu of the cave. These differences are more significant than we have been led to believe. Their importance for the dating of the Assisi series will be demonstrated in the section on the various written Legends of St. Francis.

In the meantime, it is worth noting that the representation of St. Francis in the two *Stigmatizations* is curiously dissimilar. In the Bardi Chapel, Giotto essays a prodigious contrapposto for the kneeling figure: the left knee is on the ground; below the waist, we perceive the figure as turned to the left; from the waist up, the figure twists around to the right. This vigorous—one might say Hellenistic—torsion emphasizes the saint's physical reaction to a psychical experience. He is, so to speak, magnetically pulled around from his prayer (in which he faced the *Crucifix* over the altar of Santa Croce) as he becomes aware of the mystical presence of the Seraphic Christ bearing the stigmata. Lines like threads of a spider's web search out the points of his body where the stigmata are to be implanted.

In Assisi, this posture is much simplified by eliminating the torsion. Both upper and lower parts of the body face toward the Seraphic Christ, as happened in earlier representations such as the panel now in the Bardi Chapel in Santa Croce, Florence. Quite understandably, the Assisi Master would have turned away from the energetic physicality of Giotto's figure, preferring a more tranquil and spiritualized image. It does not surprise us to discover that even in Giotto's

38. (Top) Giotto, *St. Francis Appearing to Brother Agostino and the Bishop of Assisi,* Bardi Chapel, Santa Croce, Florence

39. (Bottom) Giotto, *Stigmatization of St. Francis,* Bardi Chapel, Santa Croce, Florence

shop the simpler posture was used—as, for example, in the signed panel (Fig. 106) in the Louvre and the similar one (Fig. 107) in the Fogg Museum, Cambridge, both of which take cognizance of Giotto's fresco in other ways.

In Giotto's Bardi Chapel *Stigmatization of St. Francis,* the arched entrance to the chapel in the lower right corner is fitted with a lintel and a trefoil aperture. The small rose window and the tripartite window on the left are both treated to elaborate tracery. In several matters, then, the Assisi picture is a reduction of the one in the Bardi Chapel. On the other hand, other elements at Assisi such as the presence of Brother Leo and the second chapel may have to be explained by the newer iconography found in the St. Francis Legends of the time.

As we said at the start, the comparison between the Assisi and Bardi frescoes has seldom been a matter of primary concern or searching analysis. Just to cull a few opinions from the literature establishes this fact. For many, the relationship is already established with their attribution of the Assisi frescoes to Giotto and to an early phase of his career. This is true as well of Eve Borsook, who did not believe the Assisi series to be by Giotto but who wanted to place the Bardi Chapel frescoes earlier than the 1317 canonization of St. Louis. Her main reason was the closeness of style she detected to those in the Arena Chapel; but also, I suspect, she wanted them to be closer to Assisi which, she said, they acknowledged.[16] For Robert Oertel, the Bardi Chapel frescoes, like all other Franciscan cycles, are modeled on Assisi (even though his unknown painter of the Santa Croce scenes breaks away from that model).[17] And Dieter Blume, like Alastair Smart, saw the Assisi narratives as setting patterns and furnishing elements for Giotto's compositions in the Bardi Chapel.[18] Giovanni Previtali saw the Bardi frescoes, including the tondi in the vaults, as variants on Assisi—although his specific comparison of the two figures of St. Anthony in the *Apparition at Arles* at Assisi and in the Bardi Chapel leads Previtali to understand the path that Giotto followed, not from Assisi, but from Padua to Santa Croce.[19] And Eugenio Battisti believed that in some cases in the Bardi Chapel, Giotto "used the same cartoons as in Assisi."[20]

THE PERUZZI CHAPEL FRESCOES

The frescoes of the lives of the Baptist and St. John the Evangelist (Figs. 40–42) in the chapel next to the Bardi, that of the Peruzzi family, would seem to have no part in the dialogue between the Assisi and Santa Croce frescoes since the subject matter in the Peruzzi Chapel is different. The dating of the Peruzzi Chapel decoration is fraught with disagreement. Previtali was of the opinion that the Peruzzi frescoes were earlier than the Bardi frescoes by a number of years; he placed them around 1310–13, whereas the Bardi Chapel was done, he believed, around 1320 to 1325.[21] Previtali was followed by such critics as Bellosi, Bologna, and Boskovits.[22]

In a compelling study, Creighton Gilbert demonstrated that the two sets of frescoes were created at the same time, or rather, in alternate seasons of one year. The Peruzzi frescoes were done *a secco,* suggesting a wintertime campaign, whereas the Bardi Chapel was done in conventional fresco, suitable for a warmer season.[23] We find it difficult to believe the Peruzzi Chapel frescoes are not from a later winter, especially when we consider Offner's characterization of them: "the greater plastic swell in the figures, a fuller space, and a larger amplitude in the total effect."[24] Such sentiments were also expressed by Toesca when he spoke of "broad and spacious compositions," and remarked that "even Masaccio could learn something from them."[25]

Borsook, in the extensive study of the restoration of the Peruzzi frescoes she made with Lionello Tintori, had Giotto starting the frescoes there in 1328. One reason she wanted the Bardi Chapel frescoes earlier than the 1317 date of St. Louis' canonization was to increase the time interval between these and the considerably evolved Peruzzi frescoes.[26]

That the extraordinary spatial complexity fixes these frescoes later than those of the Bardi Chapel is amply demonstrated by both the *Ascension of St. John the Evangelist* and the *Annunciation to Zacharias* (Figs. 40 and 41). It is as though Giotto turned to the other side of the coin from the Bardi, where he had measured out such careful tensions between surface and depth resulting in those wonderfully balanced compositions that have been so much admired. In the Peruzzi Chapel, Giotto devised ways to make the composition surge out toward the spectator, using architecture and figures to build outward at the center. As a result, he was able to generate a wholly new kind of spatial dynamism. Donatello grasped Giotto's accomplishment best, as we can see in his tondi in the Old Sacristy of San Lorenzo. One is disinclined to see the accomplishment in the Peruzzi Chapel as anything but a deepening, an acceleration, and a more complex resolution of concepts begun in the Bardi Chapel. Thus the time interval observable in the frescoes themselves suggests a date for the Bardi Chapel frescoes at around 1320 and the Peruzzi in the late 1320s.

The harmoniousness of such a scene in the Bardi Chapel as the *Apparition at Arles* (Fig. 29) has been widely praised and, indeed, we have compared it to Raphael's *School of Athens.* And while Giotto's contemporaries may have admired

40. Giotto, *Ascension of St. John the Evangelist,* Peruzzi Chapel, Santa Croce, Florence

41. Giotto, *Annunciation to Zacharias,* Peruzzi Chapel, Santa Croce, Florence

these elements as much as we, they were less important to them than the things they saw in the Peruzzi Chapel work. If we take as an example the *Feast of Herod* (Fig. 42), we discover a wholly new sort of spatial envelope: the central section of the palace, the banquet hall, contains in a measured space a group of figures, one of whom, the soldier with his back to us, is cut off by the corner column and therefore serves to guide us into the scene, much as the soldier–tax collector will do later in Masaccio's *Tribute Money*. To the right, Herodias and Salome are seen in an anteroom connected to the main room by a doorway, but nicely separate from the other space and seemingly set somewhat forward from the banquet hall itself. On the left, a lone musician plays in another, separate exterior space. This keenly observed spatial presentation—complex yet highly readable— inspired the less than successful composition of the *Banquet of Herod* in Santa Maria dei Servi in Siena, a work from the shop of Pietro Lorenzetti, as well as a number of others cited by Borsook.[27] Unlike these feeble imitators, on the other hand, Ambrogio Lorenzetti in *St. Louis of Toulouse Before Pope Boniface VIII,* in

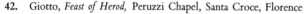

42.   Giotto, *Feast of Herod,* Peruzzi Chapel, Santa Croce, Florence

San Francesco, Siena, took vigorous advantage of this new sort of spatial complexity.

In the light of these observations, it would be useful to examine the *Miracle of the Crucifix,* scene IV (Fig. 4), in the cycle at Assisi. The structure representing San Damiano is tilted at a conspicuously odd angle, so that neither the front nor the side of the building is parallel to the ground. Can it not be interpreted as a misunderstanding of the angle of the banquet hall in the Giotto episode (in which, however, Giotto disguised the bottom architectural line that should have followed the same line as the roof)? Indeed, we see that the church in the Assisi picture is divided into two parts in quite the same way as the banquet hall. Furthermore, the right side of the scene, with the apse and crucifix, is separate and in a somewhat more forward plane than the main body of the church, again following the composition of the Peruzzi Chapel.

This episode of *St. Francis in Prayer* is furthest left in a group of three narratives, including scenes V and VI (Fig. 31). Not only are they grouped by the clusters of engaged columns to either side but, as we noted earlier, the artist has most curiously and inconsequentially symmetricized them by canting the ground line of the Lateran on the right in scene IV to the same angle as the church floor in scene IV, as though they were spatially interrelated, which, of course, they are not. Scene VI, the *Dream of Innocent III,* is itself interesting from the point of view of the structure in which the pope is placed. Such a saddleback shape is an unusual one—might not the artist have misunderstood a drawing of the *Feast of Herod* made from the Peruzzi Chapel fresco, with its garland-festooned roofline that creates, accidentally, the shape of the saddleback roof? Like the roof in the Giotto scene, the pope's roof is also bedecked with small statues set up on conspicuous plinths.

If it be not considered frivolous to trifle in such matters, it would be well to examine the roof in scene XXI (Fig. 43), *St. Francis Appearing to Brother Agostino.* Here also are the small statues set up on plinths. And, furthermore, the white steps and railings decorated with little knobs are identical to those in the upper right corner of the *Feast of Herod* in the Peruzzi Chapel. This time, however, it is no misunderstanding but a clear case of borrowing from a known source. When we look at the room below where Brother Agostino rises on his deathbed by the force of his vision (Fig. 21), we discover a rather subtler and more important borrowing from Giotto. The friars to either side are distinctly outside the space contained by the architecture, whereas Agostino is to be perceived as inside—his hands and feet are overlapped by the door frame in a conspicuous manner. Is this not an effort to imitate Giotto's soldier placed so

43. Detail of Fig. 21

conspicuously front center in his *Feast of Herod,* whose shoulder and calf are cut off by the column with such impressive spatial effect? The Assisi artist apparently grasped the idea that the soldier's figure made Giotto's space breathe.

Unless we want to believe that Giotto's development from the Bardi to the Peruzzi Chapel frescoes took place in the twinkling of an eye, it begins to look as though the artists at work on the St. Francis Legend at Assisi also had available to them the frescoes in the Peruzzi Chapel, or at least those on the wall with the Legend of St. John the Baptist. But to admit this is to admit that Giotto's frescoes in Santa Croce must be taken into account when we seek to date the cycle in the upper church, and that even such early parts of the cycle at Assisi as scenes IV to VI were not painted until the early 1330s. There are other factors that will, as we shall discover, bear out such a hypothesis.

NOTES

1. For reviews of opinions, see M. Boskovits, *Pittura fiorentina alla vigilia del Rinascimento,* Florence, 1975, 191 n. 7; for earlier opinions, such as those of Rumohr and Wickhoff, see B. Kleinschmidt, *Die Basilika San Francesco in Assisi,* 3 vols., Berlin, 1915–28, II, 1926, 151–52.

2. Not everyone has agreed to an early date. I. B. Supino (*Giotto,* 3 vols., Florence, 1920, I, 315), who attributed the frescoes to Giotto, placed them in a supposed free period from 1306 to 1310. K. Weigelt considered them to be post-Paduan (*Giotto, des Meisters Gemälde,* Stuttgart, 1925 [*Klassiker der Kunst,* vol. 29], p. L), as did Rintelen, who put them not earlier than the second decade of the fourteenth century (*Giotto und die Giotto-Apokryphen,* Munich, 1926, 181, 209).

3. Kleinschmidt, *Basilika San Francesco,* II, 158–59.

4. A. Venturi, *Storia dell'arte italiana,* V, Milan, 1907, 416.

5. R. van Marle, *The Development of the Italian Schools of Painting,* III, The Hague, 1924, 43–44.

6. H. Belting, *Oberkirche von San Francesco in Assisi, ihre Dekoration als Aufgabe und die Genese einer neuen Wandmalerei,* Berlin, 1977, 150.

7. A. Smart has a good discussion of the iconography in *The Assisi Problem and the Art of Giotto,* Oxford, 1971, 27, 200.

8. G. Previtali, *Giotto e la sua bottega,* Milan, 1967, 108.

9. P. Toesca, *Giotto,* Turin, 1941 [I grandi italiani, colla di biografie], 59.

10. R. M. Fisher, "Assisi, Padua, and the Boy in the Tree," *Art Bulletin,* XXXVIII, 1956, 47–52.

11. Smart, *Assisi Problem,* 172.

12. These will be discussed further in Chapter III; other recorded examples are illustrated in S. Waetzoldt, *Die Kopien des 17. Jahrhunderts nach Mosaiken und Wandmalerei in Rom* [Römische Forschungen der Bibliotheca Hertziana, no. 18], Vienna and Munich, 1964.

13. Smart, *Assisi Problem,* 84.

14. Van Marle, *Italian Schools,* III, Milan, 1924, 131.

15. Previtali (*Giotto,* 108) pointed out the eighteenth-century repainting of the foreshortened friar, who gazes up at St. Francis ascending.

16. Borsook, in L. Tintori and E. Borsook, *Giotto: The Peruzzi Chapel,* New York, 1963, 26.

17. R. Oertel, *Early Italian Painting to 1400,* London [ca. 1968], 111f. Oertel's belief that Giotto did not paint the Bardi Chapel frescoes was first enunciated in his review of the *Mostra giottesca* in *Zeitschrift für Kunstgeschichte,* XII, 1949, 129; see also Oertel's *Early Italian Painting,* 111–12, 185.

18. Smart, *Assisi Problem,* 164; D. Blume said that in idea and conception the Bardi Chapel *Apparition at Arles* is inspired by the one at Assisi: *Wandmalerei als Ordenspropaganda, Bildprogramme im Chorbereich franziskanischer Konvente italiens bis zur Mitte des 14. Jahrhunderts,* Worms, 1983, 61.

19. Previtali, *Giotto,* 108.

20. E. Battisti, *Giotto, Biographical and Critical Study,* Lausanne, 1960, 126.

21. Previtali, *Giotto,* 105–108, 195.

22. L. Bellosi, *Giotto,* Florence, 1981, 62; F. Bologna's dates were 1317 for the Peruzzi Chapel, and 1326–30 for the Bardi—*Novità su Giotto. Giotto al tempo della cappella Peruzzi,* Milan, 1969, 48ff. See also M. Boskovits, *Pittura fiorentina,* 191 n. 7 (with review of opinions).

23. C. Gilbert, "L'Ordine cronologico degli affreschi Bardi e Peruzzi," *Bollettino d'arte,* LIII, 1968, 192–97, with valuable insights into the time and conditions under which these frescoes were painted.

24. R. Offner, "Giotto, Non-Giotto," *Burlington Magazine,* LXXIV, 1939, 259–68; LXXV, 1939, 96–113. J. White also provided insights into the relatively advanced control of the pictorial architecture in the Peruzzi—*The Birth and Rebirth of Pictorial Space,* London, 1957, 72–77. F. Bologna so completely understood such marvels in the Peruzzi Chapel that he repeated his own paragraph on the subject from his *Novità su Giotto* in his *I pittori alla corte angioina di Napoli, 1266–1414, e un riesamo dell'arte nell'età fridericiana,* Rome, 1969, 189.

25. P. Toesca, *Florentine Painting of the Trecento,* New York, 1929, 36–37.

26. E. Borsook briefly discussed the recent literature that favored a date for the Bardi Chapel later

than the Peruzzi in *The Mural Painters of Tuscany from Cimabue to Andrea del Sarto,* New York and Oxford, 1980, 18 n. 31. As she pointed out, Previtali erred in including Pietro Toesca among those who put the Peruzzi frescoes earlier; he gives no opinion in the matter (*Il trecento* [vol. II of *Storia dell'arte italiana*], Turin, 1951, 492–93).

27. Borsook, *Peruzzi Chapel,* 10–11.

III

The Assisi Biblical Cycles

If the cycle of the St. Francis Legend had never been painted, the nave of the upper church at Assisi would still be worth a journey and would still be a mecca for lovers of art today. Arrayed along the upper walls there are a number of Old and New Testament scenes, several of which (Figs. 44–47) are, by wide accord, attributed to the important Roman artist Jacopo Torriti.[1] Beside these, there are frescoes (Figs. 49–52) by an artist who may have been the finest of Cimabue's assistants; and, of course, there are also the well-known, because more controversial, scenes (Figs. 53–55) by the so-called Isaac Master.

The date of the St. Francis Legend in the upper church at Assisi is inextricably tied to that of the Old and New Testament cycles on the upper part of the walls. No matter when the St. Francis cycle is dated, it must be at a time later than the frescoes on the walls above it. This accords with the traditional manner of painting a wall surface from top to bottom. It may be the only point of universal agreement in regard to the upper church.

To comprehend the original intention of the nave decoration in the upper church, and the way Torriti began it, we should stand at the crossing of the church and concentrate our glance on the upper scenes of the first bay to the left, that is, on the north wall: the *Creation of the World* (Fig. 44) and the *Preparation of the Ark.* Here are the grandiose effects of old Rome. For a moment one might imagine oneself back there, at St. Paul's outside the Walls or in Old St. Peter's. In the *Creation,* a majestic image of the Lord in a supernal space marked by his mandorla floats above a landscape rather like the Nilotic ones across the bottom of Torriti's *Coronation of the Virgin* (Fig. 45) in Santa Maria Maggiore and the one in his apse mosaic (redone) in St. John Lateran. The dynamic figure of the nude youth on the left and Torriti's similar figures in the border decoration of the third vault have their counterparts in the boy with the boat in his Santa Maria

44. Torriti, *Creation of the World,* Upper Church, Assisi

45. Torriti, *Coronation of the Virgin* (Detail), Mosaic, Santa Maria Maggiore, Rome

Maggiore mosaic, and they all have reference to similar early Christian figures that Torriti so much admired.[2]

The large-scaled, white-clad figures in the ark scene and, farther along, those tall, white-robed angels with Abraham (Fig. 46), all set the tone of grand Roman classicism. The narratives that start off the nave program have a grandeur entirely free of Florentine sobriety; they are unfettered by any insistence on spatial measure and clarity, but are instead endowed with that relaxed, easy looseness of space which is one of the attributes of Roman painters. There is a marked interest in grace of movement and even in ornamental refinement. Nowhere is this clearer than in the foreground of the *Wedding Feast at Cana* (Fig. 47), in the detail of the servant boys with the wine jars, the equal of which is found only in Ambrogio Lorenzetti's frescoes (Fig. 90) in the Palazzo Pubblico of Siena. The effect is strikingly different from that plastic density of forms in Cimabue's transept frescoes and from the dramatic intensity of their mood. Had the series of Old and New Testament frescoes been finished by Torriti with the same scale, color, and ease of composition with which he started, it would have constituted one of the major fresco cycles of medieval Roman painting. As it is, the admixture of succeeding shops and styles quickly destroyed any possibility of such a harmonious ensemble.

Torriti came into considerable celebrity in Rome during the 1290s, the period of his two certain works: the mosaics at the Lateran and at Santa Maria Maggiore. One might suppose that this fame, as well as the fact that he himself belonged to the Franciscan Order, would have made him the ideal choice to begin the nave decoration at Assisi. Although Julian Gardner in his invaluable study of Torriti's work for Nicholas IV was convinced that Torriti was in Assisi in the late 1280s, it is more likely that he was there after the fall of the Colonna put an end to his work in Santa Maria Maggiore in 1297.[3] The frescoes he designed and painted at Assisi appear to be those of a mature artist working in a rather loose and relaxed manner. Theories that would put his work back into earlier decades—even to the 1260s by one accounting—lack persuasiveness.[4] In all probability, Torriti was working in the upper church at the turn of the century, that is, after his Roman triumphs at Santa Maria Maggiore and St. John Lateran.

The work on the nave walls would in normal circumstances have proceeded from bay to bay, commencing at the crossing and proceeding toward the entrance wall. Thus, if the scaffolding was in place in the fourth bay (counting from the entrance) for both sides of the nave, Torriti would have worked on the first Creation scenes on the right, or north, wall and the *Annunciation* and the *Wedding Feast at Cana* on the left, or south, wall.[5] In the *Annunciation,* the figures

46. (Top) Torriti, *Abraham and the Three Angels* (Detail), Upper Church, Assisi

47. (Bottom) Torriti, *Wedding Feast at Cana,* Upper Church, Assisi

closely relate to those of Torriti's mosaic of the subject in Santa Maria Maggiore of the mid-1290s. The niche-throne, on the other hand, has become much more architectural—a foreshortened side of a building relates to the column, capital, and lintel of the niche where the Virgin stands in the Roman mosaic. Later we will discuss the further spatial development Torriti produced in the *Wedding Feast at Cana* just below the *Annunciation*.

If Torriti's selection for the Assisi work and his commencement of it were deliberate, so, it appears, was his departure precipitous. Altogether he seems to have painted the upper level of the fourth bay on either side and then the third bay on the north side. Thereafter, Torriti proceeded along the nave to the second bay and painted the *Expulsion from Paradise* (Fig. 48) in the upper left side. We do not know about the lost companion scene across the window in that bay, but we can say that his work terminated here because the very next scenes are those just below, in such a different manner, by the Isaac Master.

In the meantime, across the nave in the third and second bays, an important but anonymous Cimabuesque painter designed and painted the New Testament episodes from the *Nativity* (Fig. 49) to the *Crucifixion*.[6] This probably occurred at the same time as Torriti was at work. Stylistic factors everywhere announce the Cimabue modes: the Virgin's head in the *Presentation*, Christ's head in the *Betrayal* (Fig. 50), the angels of the *Nativity*, and, as much as anything, the Prophet heads in the border decoration of several bays, including the fourth bay flanking Torriti's Creation scenes (Figs. 51 and 52). These frescoes of the third and second bays have been variously attributed, sometimes to Torriti, sometimes to a Cimabuesque. There seems little doubt that they should be considered along with the best work of Cimabue's workshop, as can be determined by the closeness of style to the fine *Enthroned Madonna* in the Louvre, possibly by the same artist.[7]

In recent times, the literature has concentrated on two episodes from the Old Testament cycle in the upper church, the *Deception of Isaac* (Fig. 53) and the *Esau Before Isaac* (Fig. 54), in the second bay from the entrance on the right, or north, wall of the church. The anonymous artist of these scenes, commonly called the Isaac Master, has in the last few years increasingly been identified with the young Giotto. For those who also attribute the St. Francis cycle to the same hand that did the two Isaac scenes, Giotto does indeed, as Belting put it, dominate the nave of the upper church.[8]

We should not be too firm about the period in which the Isaac Master worked until we undertake to study what it was that preceded his work on the walls of the upper church. The literature on this subject is itself vast and cannot be gone into thoroughly here. Suffice to say that since Millard Meiss, in a short

48. Second Bay, Right Wall, Upper Church, Assisi

49. Cimabue Follower, *Nativity,* Upper Church, Assisi

50. Cimabue Follower, *Betrayal,* Upper Church, Assisi

51. Cimabue Follower, *Prophet,* Upper Church, Assisi

52. Cimabue Follower, *Prophet,* Upper Church, Assisi

53. Isaac Master, *Deception of Isaac,* Upper Church, Assisi   54. Isaac Master, *Esau Before Isaac,* Upper Church, Assisi

treatment of the theme, assigned the Isaac scenes to the youthful Giotto in a pre-Paduan period, a large number of the scholars concerned have given their assent to his proposition.[9] Thus, for some, an easy progression emerges in Giotto's oeuvre: from the Isaac scenes to the St. Francis Legend to the series in the Arena Chapel in Padua. Thus also, the Isaac Master, once the "great unknown," to quote Oertel, becomes Giotto.[10] And Meiss could write that "if the Isaac Master is not Giotto, then he and not Giotto is the founder of modern painting."[11] For Smart, the two scenes are unsurpassed in the upper church decoration, "the product of a sublime and profound mind."[12] And although Nicholson did not agree that the Isaac Master was Giotto, his praise of the former was extravagant: he considered the Isaac Master the greatest painter of the Roman school.[13]

On the other hand, the case for him has surely been exaggerated. The nearly perfect measure and the frozen orderliness of these two compositions do not necessarily speak to their originality. Furthermore, the incised lines found by Tintori in the *Lamentation* (Fig. 55) suggest a carefully pre-planned composition, the like of which cannot be found in, for example, Giotto's Arena Chapel series.[14]

In the *Esau Before Isaac* (Fig. 54), the old father raises himself up on his bed like an ancient river god, and both he and the other protagonists hold their

55. Isaac Master, *Lamentation,* Upper
Church, Assisi

poses with an unbreathing stiffness we would expect of mannequins. Their
draperies fall in razor-sharp folds and cluster ostentatiously around several radial
points. All the surfaces—as of draperies and hair—have a shiny, lapidary quality
that is most easily apprehended in the beard of Isaac. The artist works in plastic
masses: the density of the oval heads is as remarkable as the clearly carved faces.
These figures are too much statues to be capable of life and movement. All of
these stylistic features are effectively used by the Isaac Master in his dreamlike
tableaux that emphasize so well the dark tensions of the narrative.

It is very probable that the Isaac scenes owe something to preexistent
models such as those by Giotto in the Arena Chapel, although, as we shall see,
there are other possible sources for him. The room space in which both of the
Isaac narratives are set is of an advanced and sophisticated type: the front side of
the room is parallel to the picture plane, while the side is canted back on a
diagonal from the corner column, affording a view into the room from its side.[15]
It is more evolved than Giotto's earliest interiors in the Arena Chapel as, for
example, the arrangement in the *Birth of the Virgin* (Fig. 56). On the other hand,
it more nearly resembles the solution Giotto arrived at in the *Last Supper,* or the
Pentecost (Fig. 57), in which the interior swells up to fill almost all of the picture
space. Looked at this way, we would want to say that the Isaac Master derived
such a new spatial concept from Giotto after the Paduan frescoes had been painted.

One of the marvels of the Arena Chapel series, of course, is the sense
Giotto conveys of the figures really occupying the three-dimensional space into

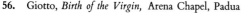

56. Giotto, *Birth of the Virgin*, Arena Chapel, Padua   57. Giotto, *Pentecost*, Arena Chapel, Padua

which he sets them. It is quite the contrary with the Isaac Master: even though the space is cunningly contrived, it lacks the proper dimensionality to hold the figures. They appear to coexist with the interior but not to occupy it, which may be a Roman factor. Certainly it recalls the figure-to-space relationship in Cavallini, as in the mosaics in Santa Maria in Trastevere (Fig. 58), or the lost frescoes from St. Paul's outside the Walls, Rome, known to us from old drawings (Figs. 59 and 60).[16] The involvement in spaces that contain figures is very much a Tuscan predilection, as we see so well in Giotto, but it seldom reaches the same importance in the Roman school. Here, as in so many other matters, the Roman nature of the Isaac Master betrays itself. Consequently, we are especially interested in the relationship to Cavallini's art.

   We will have a clearer idea of what the Cavallini type of setting was —and consequently of what the Isaac Master inherited—if we examine the characteristics of Cavallini's compositions in St. Paul's outside the Walls, or that part of the program for which we believe he was responsible, that is, the Old Testament scenes.[17] Although the literature has generally discussed both the Old Testament wall and the opposite wall with the *Acts of the Apostles* as the work of Cavallini, this is surely not so.[18] Clearly two artists, and two generations, faced one another across the nave of St. Paul's. In the New Testament scenes (Figs. 61 and 62), postures are strenuously energetic: one leg is usually raised off the ground whether the figure is running, standing, or sitting. Arms are frequently outstretched, expressing a variety of states of mind. Torsos bend forward or back or

58. (Left) Cavallini, *Nativity of the Virgin,* Mosaic, Santa Maria in Trastevere, Rome

59. (Below) *Massacre of the Egyptian Firstborn,* Sketch, Ms. Barb. Lat. 4406, Fo. 56ʳ, Vatican, Rome

60. *Joseph with Potiphar's Wife,* Sketch, Ms. Barb. Lat. 4406, Fo. 48ʳ, Vatican, Rome

61. (Above) *Flagellation of St. Paul,* Sketch, Ms. Barb. Lat. 4406, Fo. 100ʳ, Vatican, Rome

62. (Right) *Flight Before the Apotheosis in Lystra,* Sketch, Ms. Barb. Lat., 4406, Fo. 114ʳ, Vatican, Rome

twist. Nothing could be more contrary to all this than what we see in the Old Testament illustrations across the nave: even striding figures have both feet on the ground; figures tend to sit or stand in a more vertical position, and arms frequently bend at the elbow, restraining the gesture.

There are other differences. The *Acts of the Apostles* is characterized by the most vivid sorts of structures and by the variety of the mise-en-scènes. One must admit that the background settings amaze us with their splendor, their variety and complexity. Temples abound, both rectangular and round, both drapery-festooned and plain, peripteral and pseudo-peripteral; there are arcades both gabled and pointed, as well as fortifications with and without crenellations. One finds a basilica interior with a gallery of short columns along the upper level, another with a clerestory and engaged columns with arched openings on the side.[19] Often the architectural elements jostle one another so that, in one scene, Barnabas ostentatiously collides with the jamb of an arched city gate.

Much of this is rich and sophisticated, out of the old and learned Roman tradition, an important precedent being the frescoes in San Clemente, Rome—and, in fact, there are instances in San Paolo of something like the garlanded sets of the San Clemente frescoes of the late eleventh century.[20] At other times, the early Christian spirit asserts itself—we remember the explicitly characterized "imperial" Roman architecture in the fourth-century mosaic at Santa Pudenziana.[21] Even with these recollections of early Christian art, there is no evidence in the seventeenth-century drawings that the *Acts of the Apostles* was not entirely repainted in the thirteenth century. We know that the draughtsman caught such stylistic differences very precisely: in the last ten episodes of the Old Testament series, which are the original early Christian paintings (Figs. 63 and 64), the

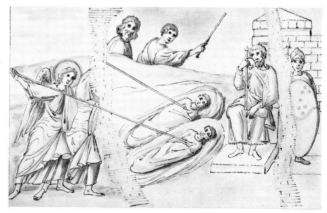

63. (Above) *Abraham Departs with Offering,* Sketch, Ms. Barb. Lat. 4406, Fo. 39, Vatican, Rome

64. (Right) *Massacre of the Egyptian Firstborn,* Sketch, Ms. Barb. Lat. 4406, Fo.62ʳ, Vatican, Rome

copyist knew to render the short and stocky proportions of the figures. The "architecture" is given as uncomplicated cubic shapes behind the figures, and the horizon is a uniformly straight line three-quarters up in the scene.[22]

What we see in those New Testament scenes is exactly what Cavallini would not have done since he was himself so reticent in his architectural settings. For example, in the Old Testament series, he has Pharaoh sit in the simplest aedicula in the scene of the *Massacre of the Egyptian Firstborn* (Fig. 59),[23] yet his figure is well contained within it. In the *Miracle of the Snakes,* the integration of figures and settings is, as Julian Gardner pointed out, more accomplished than anything in the New Testament side of the nave.

It is interesting to see how the setting for the narratives at St. Paul's that Cavallini repainted fits into the artist's oeuvre. In the *Massacre of the Egyptian Firstborn* and the *Joseph with Potiphar's Wife* (Figs. 59 and 60), one with an aedicula-throne, the other with foreshortened side walls, their cubic density serves to anchor the figures in space—as, indeed, Cavallini would also do in the *Nativity of the Virgin* (Fig. 58) in Santa Maria in Trastevere. In each instance, Cavallini used the setting to enhance the sculptural relief of his figures. This is very similar to the way he used a number of small but space-generating "doorway" and throne structures in all his Trastevere mosaics, so that the logical progression of his art from the 1280s to the 1290s is observable.

It is not the tradition represented by the New Testament series in St. Paul's outside the Walls that the Isaac Master followed, but rather the Old Testament cycle of his one-time master, Cavallini. And very specifically, as we have already noted, the Isaac Master culled elements from such a Cavallini mosaic as the *Nativity of the Virgin* at Santa Maria in Trastevere. One cannot fail to be impressed with the similarity of the arrangements in the Isaac scenes (Figs. 53 and 54) at Assisi: the patterned wall hangings, the bed with arcaded front side, the two stiffly posed figures behind the bed (their gestures the reverse of those in the Roman work). One imagines that this scene directly inspired the composition of the Isaac Master in Assisi. On the other hand, the Isaac Master's architectural setting for the two Isaac scenes is evolutionarily well in advance of Cavallini's in Santa Maria in Trastevere, as we have observed in the analysis of his architectural setting for the two Isaac scenes.

We have discussed the way in which the Isaac Master's compositional setting is close to that of the advanced stage of Giotto's thinking in the Arena Chapel frescoes. Two other frescoes of the same era may help us to fix the evolutionary stage of the Isaac Master. One of these is the *Deception of Isaac* (Fig. 65) on the right wall of Santa Cecilia, Rome. This is one of several Old and New

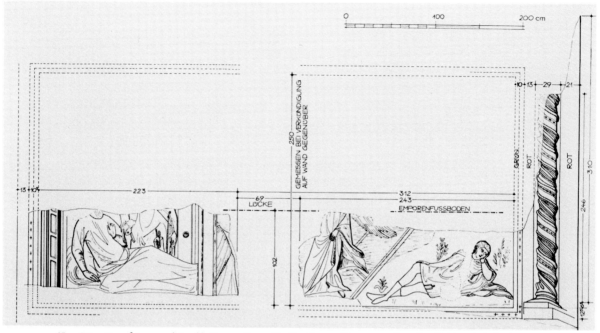

65. *Deception of Isaac* and *Jacob's Dream,* Santa Cecilia, Rome, Reconstruction after Belting *(Oberkirche von Assisi)*

Testament scenes that survive from what must have been two more extensive nave cycles. Beside this scene is *Jacob's Dream,* while across the nave on the opposite wall we have a part of the *Annunciation.* [24] These frescoes have generally been taken to be the work of Cavallini's assistants or followers, and the assumption has been that they were executed at the same time as the *Last Judgment* on the entrance wall.[25] If indeed they were, we can be all the surer that it was a younger colleague of Cavallini's with newer ideas of composition. The *Deception of Isaac* has an architectural arrangement that has nothing to do with Cavallini's art in the 1290s: on the right side of the scene, the architecture recedes on a diagonal and has a large open area through which a figure is seen entering the room. The very sophistication of this presentation is evolutionarily in advance of Cavallini.

The Santa Cecilia fresco should be compared to the experimentations that Giotto was making with such arrangements of figures cut off by architectural parts, especially in his *Birth of the Virgin* (Fig. 56) in Padua, in which the porch constitutes such a diagonally placed "room" and in which the corner column bisects the entering neighbor. With these examples in mind, we should also consider the *Wedding Feast at Cana* (Fig. 47) in the fourth bay, south wall, of the nave at Assisi, which we attribute to Torriti. The column, capital, and lintel constitute the right corner of a room whose side recedes on an angle. It is true that the table at which the gathering sits is not properly contained within the space of this room, and it is true that the servant boy will not easily navigate an entry into the room from the side. Nevertheless, this open room with foreshortened side is the architectural and spatial breakthrough we have already observed in two other places: the Arena Chapel in Padua and the Isaac scenes farther along the nave at Assisi.

We can be sure that the Isaac scenes followed Torriti's *Wedding Feast at Cana* inasmuch as the work proceeded down the nave from the crossing to the entrance. One begins to suspect that the motif of the figure in the doorway was a newly popular one in the beginning of the fourteenth century, just for its space-generating possibilities. Its presence in Torriti's fresco encourages us to date his work in Assisi to the first decade of the fourteenth century, that is, at the same time as Giotto's Arena Chapel frescoes. Secondly, it is clear that such well-developed spatial forays go beyond what Cavallini had achieved in St. Paul's outside the Walls,[26] or at Santa Maria in Trastevere; while, lastly, there is no reason to suppose this advance had been formulated by the Isaac Master himself. Curiously, the figure outside the doorway in the *Esau Before Isaac* (Fig. 54) makes no attempt to cross the threshold. In that sense, measuring the situation from several angles, we must conclude that the Isaac Master was to a large extent derivative.

The kinship between Cavallini, the painter of the nave frescoes in Santa Cecilia, and the Isaac Master is remarkably strong. Some essential points of style in the Isaac scenes resemble those in the *Annunciation* (Fig. 66) in Santa Cecilia: the stiff poses and gestures, the overly-clear ovoid shape of the heads, as well as the hard, carved features.[27] If the Isaac Master was, as we suppose, a pupil of Cavallini, he would have been that much younger, and consequently well advanced from the evolutionary stage of Cavallini (as we have detailed above in the discussion of the architectural settings he employed). He reminds us, in fact, of another Roman artist—one who seems to have worked on part of the St. Benedict Legend at the Sacro Speco in Subiaco and who may likewise have been a pupil of Cavallini, perhaps working at the same time as the Isaac Master at Assisi.[28]

Of course, the Isaac Master may have commenced work immediately after Torriti ceased his own (Fig. 48). Yet there is the sense that some time elapsed so that when work recommenced, it was no longer so essential to follow in the footsteps of Torriti or, for that matter, the Cimabuesque artist; that is to say, little need or desire to continue in "the old style." There can be no denying that the

66. Cavallini Follower, *Annunciation,* Santa Cecilia, Rome

direction of the work at Assisi underwent a fundamental change. It is easier to understand this difference when we realize that the Isaac Master was not on the scene until the second decade of the fourteenth century. For example, a certain sophistication in the handling of those architectural forms is what we might expect from an artist of a younger generation and after the lapse of possibly several years.

To an extent, the Isaac Master's mode of work and temperament had an effect on the part of the program entrusted to him. Beside the two famous Isaac scenes, this master also painted most of the narratives in the first bay nearest the entrance on either side of the nave.[29] It was not, apparently, an easy progression, nor was it, in all probability, continuous and uninterrupted. He was much assisted by mediocre pupils, and the master appears not to have maintained total control. Thus in the *Lamentation* (Fig. 55), in which the face, hair, and drapery of St. John the Evangelist are the master's own creation, most of the other figures are not very successful and the picture as a whole is disorganized. No wonder it brought Rintelen's frostiest but most humorous remark to the effect that the Christ figure lies on his side with a hand and foot near the bottom edge so that his body seems almost to be tipping over.[30] In the episodes of *Joseph and His Brothers* and the *Twelve Year Old Christ in the Temple,* these problems are compounded by the overbearing architecture pressing down upon the figures and the space.

We would not want to say that the Isaac Master was the author of the paired saint figures on the archway tangential to the entrance wall or of the church *Doctors* in the first vault. These are much more developed, and they contain more Gothic characteristics than anything in the narrative cycles in the nave. In them we see painters artistically akin to the Isaac Master but working at a later time.[31] We must suppose that the lapse before this part of the work was accomplished would carry us up to a period closer to the middle of the fourteenth century; no doubt they were the last things to be executed in the upper church nave. Their similarity to comparable vault decoration and images of saints that appear in a good many Riminese paintings of the midcentury is surprisingly close, especially those at Tolentino.[32]

What is most illuminating about the analysis of the Old and New Testament frescoes in the upper church at Assisi is the realization that in no instance, not even in the work of the Isaac Master, do we discover any element of the new vernacular approach that is the very cornerstone of the St. Francis cycle in the same church. Like the work of his one-time master, Cavallini, even in the 1308 frescoes at San Domenico, Naples, and like Giotto in Padua and in the Magdalen Chapel of the lower church, the Old and New Testament paintings at Assisi follow the idealizing and monumentalizing narrative manner inherited from the thirteenth-century art of Italy and from the earlier grand traditions in Rome and in Byzantium. Thus the step from the Isaac Master's frescoes to the St. Francis cycle is a prodigious one, at once bringing us into a modern world with an entirely new set of pictorial values, of which we have had just glimpses in the frescoes and mosaics of Rome.

Indeed, there appears to have been a new art emergent in Rome after the Isaac Master, of which we have several outstanding examples. One of these is the frescoes in the narthex of San Lorenzo outside the Walls, which include the legends of St. Lawrence and of St. Stephen and the Golden Chalice.[33] While these are generally dated to the end of the Dugento, further study might reveal them to be well into the fourteenth century. When we examine the *Condemnation and Decapitation of St. Romanus* and *Decius Condemns St. Lawrence to Death* (Fig. 67), we know that the trustworthiness of these much-repainted frescoes is proven by comparing them to the old sketches made of them (Fig. 68). We have to agree with Guglielmo Matthiae in his description of them as part of a new "popular" art.[34] He wrote of the vivacity of movement, the complexity of the spaces, and

67. (Above) *Condemnation and Decapitation of St. Romanus* and *Decius Condemns St. Lawrence to Death,* St. Lawrence outside the Walls, Rome

68. (Left) *Condemnation and Decapitation of St. Romanus,* Sketch, Ms. Barb. Lat. 4403, 18^r, Vatican, Rome

the preoccupation with fashionable costumes, as well as the unconstrained *(sbrigliata)* narrative. To us, all of this suggests fourteenth-century attitudes, that is to say, attitudes that most likely sprang up in the 1320s and 1330s.

Finally, a discussion of the new trends in Roman painting in the early fourteenth century must include the mosaics on the facade of Santa Maria Maggiore in Rome. We do not refer to the old-fashioned, Dugentesque enthroned Redeemer and Saints (Fig. 69), signed by Rusuti and bearing the date 1308. That work has nothing in common with the scenes below concerning Pope Liberius and the building of the basilica.[35] Matthiae himself described these Liberian scenes

69. (Above) Old Facade of Santa Maria Maggiore, Rome, Sketch, National Gallery of Scotland, Edinburgh

70. (Left) *The Patrician Giovanni Offering Pope Liberius a New Basilica,* Mosaic, Santa Maria Maggiore, Rome

as having complex architecture, unconstrained vivacity of postures, and attentive study of costumes. Indeed, such an episode as *The Patrician Giovanni Offering Pope Liberius a New Basilica* (Fig. 70) has about it a striking air of modernity, which places it later than the older, formalized mosaics by Rusuti in the zone above, and which can scarcely be conceived of before the late 1320s.[36]

It would be difficult to see the Isaac Master's oeuvre in the same light. We must understand him as being of a younger generation than Cavallini, but at the same time of an older generation than that which worked—possibly as late as the 1330s—on the San Lorenzo Frescoes and the Santa Maria Maggiore facade mosaics. One cannot escape the conclusion that so radical a difference as that found in Torriti and Cimabue's shop and then in the Isaac Master forces us to see all three as old-fashioned precedents, separated by more than a few years from the new style of the St. Francis cycle.

NOTES

1. In the older literature, the entire series of Old and New Testament scenes could be attributed to Pietro Cavallini (A. Venturi, *Storia dell'arte italiana,* V, Milan, 1907, 178–79), and F. Bologna could give the first Creation scenes to Rusuti (*Early Italian Painting, Romanesque and Early Medieval Art,* Rome, 1964, 97). I. B. Supino (*La Basilica di San Francesco d'Assisi,* Bologna, 1924, 104–10) assiged the two bays nearest the crossing to Torriti, as did van Marle in *La peinture romaine au moyen-âge, son développement du 6ème jusqu'à la fin du 13ème siècle,* Strasbourg, 1921, 219–20. So, too, did Matthiae in *Pittura romana del medioevo,* II, Rome, 1966, ch. V, 217–28, esp. 225, excluding the scenes in the third bay on the left. C. Volpe is one of those who demurred. He attributed the *Building the Ark* and the *Sacrifice of Isaac* to a Cimabuesque Tuscan master, whereas he saw the immobile Torriti as responsible for some of the Creation scenes in the sluggish Roman manner ("La formazione di Giotto nella cultura di Assisi," in *Giotto e i giotteschi,* ed. G. Palumbo, Rome, 1969, 15–59, esp. 34).

2. P. Hetherinton demonstrated the influence of early Christian art on Torriti in "Pietro Cavallini, Artistic Style and Patronage in Late Medieval

Rome," *Burlington Magazine,* CXIV, 1972, 4–10. According to H. Henkels, "Remarks on the Late XIII Century Apse Decoration in Santa Maria Maggiore," *Simiolus,* IV, 1971, 128–49, the section of mosaic called the "Shores of Paradise" along the bottom of the *Coronation of the Virgin* with its array of animals, birds, and putti was lifted out of the original apse mosaic and reused here by Torriti. C. Cecchelli, in his *I mosaici della basilica di S. Maria Maggiore* (Turin, 1956, 246–52), dwelt on Torriti's apparently assiduous copying of the early Christian apse mosaic with its Nilotic landscape, which he was replacing without any mention of his use of part of it, even though the issue had been raised years before by A. Schuchert (*S. Maria Maggiore zu Rom. Die Grundungsgeschichte der Basilika und die ursprüngliche Apsisanlage,* Vatican City, 1939, 119). See also W. Oakeshott, *The Mosaics of Rome,* Greenwich, Conn., 1967, 94. But Boskovits disagreed with the Henkel theory ("Nuovi studi su Giotto e Assisi," *Paragone,* no. 261, 1971, 34–56, esp. 49 n. 11).

3. J. Gardner, "Pope Nicholas IV and the Decoration of Santa Maria Maggiore," *Zeitschrift für Kunstgeschichte,* XXXVI, 1973, 39. J. White also believed the Assisi frescoes preceded the Santa Maria Mag-

giore work of the 1290s: *Art and Architecture in Italy, 1250 to 1400,* Baltimore, 1966, 133.

4. M. Boskovits, "Nuovi studi su Giotto e Assisi," *Paragone,* no. 261, 1971, 37, 49 n. 10; I. Hueck, "Der Maler der Apostelszenen im Atrium von Alt-St. Peter," *Mitteilungen des kunsthistorischen Institutes in Florenz,* XIV, 1969, 143–44.

5. The Torriti episodes on the north wall are the following: the *Creation of the World,* the *Creation of Adam,* the *Creation of Eve,* the *Temptation of Adam and Eve,* the *Fall of Man,* the *Building of the Ark,* the *Sacrifice of Abraham, Abraham and the Three Angels;* the scene just to the right of the *Expulsion,* possibly the *Labor of Adam and Eve,* was also probably the work of Torriti and his shop, and seems to have been the last he executed in Assisi. On the south wall, Torriti painted the *Annunciation,* the mostly destroyed *Visitation,* the *Wedding Feast at Cana,* and the *Resurrection of Lazarus.*

6. These eight scenes include the *Nativity,* the *Adoration of the Magi,* the *Presentation in the Temple,* the *Flight into Egypt,* the *Betrayal,* the *Flagellation,* the *Via Crucis,* and the *Crucifixion.*

7. Volpe especially found the Cimabuesque to be a still controlling force at the beginning of the nave decoration ("La formazione di Giotto nella cultura di Assisi," in *Giotto e i giotteschi,* 15–59, esp. 34). Essentially, Volpe was continuing the Longhian thesis, in which Duccio was seen as a Cimabue assistant at Assisi, painting among other things much of the *Crucifixion* (R. Longhi, "Giudizio sul duecento," *Proporzioni,* II, 1948, 5–54). See also F. Bologna, "Ciò che resta di un capolavoro giovanile di Duccio," *Paragone,* no. 125, 1960, 3–31; and C. Volpe, "Preistoria di Duccio," *Paragone,* no. 49, 1954, 4–22.

8. H. Belting, *Oberkirche von San Francesco in Assisi: ihre Dekoration als Aufgabe und die Genese einer neuen Wandmalerei,* Berlin, 1977, 142.

9. M. Meiss, *Giotto and Assisi,* New York, 1960. A recent dissenter is C. Brandi, who returned these two scenes once again to the Roman school (*Giotto,* Milan, 1983, 16).

10. R. Oertel, *Early Italian Painting to 1400,* London [ca. 1968], 67.

11. Meiss, *Giotto and Assisi,* 25.

12. A. Smart, *The Assisi Problem and the Art of Giotto,* Oxford, 1971, 117.

13. A. Nicholson, "The Roman School at Assisi," *Art Bulletin,* XII, 1930, 270–300.

14. L. Tintori and M. Meiss, *The Paintings of the Life of St. Francis in Assisi,* New York, 1960, 16.

15. J. White discussed the Isaac Master's improvement of the foreshortened frontal system over that in the *Supper at Cana* in *The Birth and Rebirth of Pictorial Space,* London, 1957, 32.

16. The Vatican manuscript, Barb. Lat. 4406; see S. Waetzoldt, *Die Kopien des 17. Jahrhunderts nach Mosaiken und Wandmalerei in Rom* [Römische Forschungen der Bibliotheca Hertziana, no. 18], Vienna and Munich, 1964, 55–64, figs. 328–408.

17. For Pietro Cavallini's work at St. Paul's, see P. Hetherington, *Pietro Cavallini: A Study in the Art of Late Medieval Rome,* London, 1979, ch. VII, 81–106, with charts of the narratives; G. Matthiae, *Pietro Cavallini,* Rome, 1972, ch. IV, 39–52, also with lists of titles for the individual episodes; J. White, "Cavallini and the Lost Frescoes in S. Paolo," *Journal of the Warburg and Courtauld Institutes,* XIX, 1956, 844–95; and J. Gardner, "S. Paolo fuori le mura, Nicholas III, and Pietro Cavallini," *Zeitschrift für Kunstgeschichte,* XXIV, 1971, 240–48. For illustrations of the seventeenth-century drawings in the Vatican codex Barb. Lat. 4406, and complete listing of titles, see Waetzoldt, *Kopien nach Mosaiken,* 55–61, figs. 328–407.

18. Gardner, in the article cited, "S. Paolo fuori le mura," proposed that Cavallini was a pupil of an older Roman master and helped on the *Acts of the Apostles.*

19. For other illustrations, see Waetzoldt, *Kopien nach Mosaiken,* figs. 366, 378, and 391.

20. Matthiae, *Pittura Romana,* II, figs. 11–13 and color plates opposite pp. 32, 36, and 40.

21. Ibid., I, fig. 29.

22. For illustrations of the other unrepainted narratives, see Waetzoldt, *Kopien nach Mosaiken,* figs. 343–45, 360–64.

23. Ibid., fig. 358.

24. See the diagram on p. 159 in Belting, *Oberkirche von San Francesco.* Illustrated in Matthiae, *Pietro Cavallini,* plates LXXVI–LXXVII; and in Hetherington, *Pietro Cavallini,* figs. 69–71, 74–75.

25. Hetherington, *Pietro Cavallini,* 39; Bertelli, "Mostra degli affreschi di Grottaferrata," *Paragone,* no. 249, 1970, 94; Toesca, *Pietro Cavallini,* Milan,

1959, London, 1960, 14. For Belting, the framing elements of these scenes represented "Cavallini's decorative system," but this can hardly be accepted given our knowledge of his work in the 1290s (*Oberkirche von San Francesco,* 158).

26. In this sense, it is perhaps too easy to exaggerate the progressiveness of the scene of *Joseph and Potiphar's Wife* (Fig. 60); see "Cavallini and the Lost Frescoes," 90–92.

27. Illustrated in Matthiae, *Cavallini,* 1972, plate LXXVI. See also the Cavallinesque frescoes in Santa Maria in Trastevere illustrated by Parronchi, "Attività del 'Maestro di Santa Cecilia'," *Rivista d'arte,* XXI, 1939, figs. 4–7.

28. Both Hermanin and Matthiae gave good accounts of the Subiaco frescoes except that, in the traditional manner, all the frescoes were seen as the product of one hand—Federigo Hermanin, "Le pitture dei monasteri sublacensi," in *I monasteri di Subiaco,* ed. P. Egidi, 2 vols., Rome, 1904, 464–72; Matthiae, *Pittura romana,* 239–43. Stephan Wolohojian is preparing a study of the St. Benedict Legend in the Sacro Speco.

29. We may suppose that his contribution consisted of the *Sacrifice of Cain and Abel* (destroyed), the *Cain Killing Abel, Joseph Lowered into the Well, Joseph and His Brothers,* all on the north wall; and on the south wall, the *Twelve Year Old Christ Child Disputing with the Elders,* the *Baptism of Christ,* the *Lamentation,* and *The Three Marys at the Tomb.* The *Pentacost* and the *Ascension* on the entrance wall cannot be associated with the Isaac Master; their relationship is, rather, to the St. Francis Legend on the nave walls.

30. F. Rintelen, *Giotto und die Giotto-Apokryphen,* Munich, 1926, 82. Recently, C. Brandi, in attributing the picture to a follower of Giotto, was still able to speak of it as the "grand event" of the New Testament cycle (*Giotto,* Milan, 1983, 24).

31. For commentaries on the complexities of the spaces in the *Doctor* webs and on the probable lateness of the work, see White, *Birth and Rebirth,* 31, and L. Lochoff, "Gli affreschi dell'antico e nuovo testamento nella basilica superiore di Assisi," *Rivista d'arte* XVI, 1937, 262. F. Bologna in *I pittori alla corte angioina di Napoli, 1266–1414, e un riesamo dell'arte nell'età fridericiana,* Rome, 1969, 108–109, identifying the painter of these frescoes with Giotto, had him finishing all the nave paintings. For G. Previtali, the paired saints on the under arch contiguous to the facade wall are Giotto's earliest work at Assisi; according to Previtali, Giotto was assisted in the thirty-three half figures by Memmo di Filippuccio (*Giotto e la sua bottega,* Milan, 1967, 43). For good illustrations, see L. Coletti, *Gli affreschi della Basilica di Assisi,* Bergamo, 1949, plates 56–59.

32. For the best illustrations of the Tolentino frescoes, see C. Volpe, *La pittura riminese del Trecento,* Milan, 1965, cat. no. 92.

33. E. Muñoz, *La basilica di S. Lorenzo,* Rome [1944]; G. Matthiae, *S. Lorenzo fuori le mura,* Rome, 1966, 63–73.

34. Matthiae, *Pittura romana,* 188–89; idem, "Le arte plastiche e figurative," in *Arte, scienze e cultura in Roma cristiana,* by Mariano da Alatri, Isidoro da Villapadierna, and others, Bologna, 1971, 53.

35. Matthiae distinguished between Rusuti's mosaic and the Liberian ones, reminding us that Vasari had attributed these later ones to Gaddo Gaddi ("Le arti plastiche e figurative," 55).

36. Gardner recognized the difference between the Rusuti work and the Liberian narratives. But inasmuch as the pope had (rather famously) lost the great ruby from his papal tiara in Lyons in 1305, Gardner reasoned that the mosaic at Santa Maria Maggiore in which the ruby is clearly seen must predate the 1305 incident—"Pope Nicholas IV," 32–33.

IV

Problems in the Dating of the Assisi Cycle

There is no firm evidence of a date, early or late, for the St. Francis cycle in the upper church at Assisi. Of the variety of supposedly evidential material put forward to persuade us of an early date, none has ultimately proved convincing. Vasari, for example, gave out that the frescoes were done at the behest of Giovanni di Muro della Marca when he was General of the Franciscan Order (1296–1305), and this is sometimes even taken to be fact, apparently on Vasari's say-so.[1] Vasari's supposition cannot ever have been more than that.

Much store is put by the passage in the *Compilatio chronologica* of Riccobaldo Ferrarese, who died in 1319, and whose political, military, and ecclesiastical compendium was probably written between 1312–13 and 1318–19.[2] This well-known passage, frequently repeated in the literature, cited the places Giotto painted, including the Arena Chapel, Padua, as well as the Minorite (that is, the Franciscan) churches of Assisi, Rimini, and Padua. The reference to Assisi is generally thought to concern the St. Francis cycle in the upper church—an especially strong weapon for those who would defend Giotto's authorship of the series and an early date. It is quite possible that Riccobaldo knew for certain that Giotto was involved in these places, especially if, like Dante, he knew the artist personally. Certainly the works in which we believe Giotto had been involved by 1312—those in Padua and the Magdalen Chapel (Figs. 71 and 72) in the lower church at Assisi—give a not inaccurate view of his major accomplishments up to that time.

The *Compilatio* is generally described as being an account of kings and popes, of weighty matters of state in which the appearance of a comment about

71. (Top) Giotto Shop, *Noli Me Tangere,* Magdalen Chapel, Lower Church, Assisi

72. (Left) Giotto, *Magdalen with Bishop Pontano,* Magdalen Chapel, Lower Church, Assisi

an artist would have appeared almost frivolous. Indeed, it has been suggested that it is a relatively unique phenomenon in fourteenth-century historical chronicles, so that it can only be explained by the possibility that the author knew Dante's *Purgatorio,* in which the famous Florentine artist is mentioned.[3] On the other hand, a perusal of the *Compilatio* reveals what a heterogeneous clustering of facts it is. Three entries past the Giotto one is a description of the damage from a "terraemotus magnus Arimini." A few items farther on, Riccobaldo tells us of a "solis eclipsis non magna." Still farther along, toward the end, observation of a comet in January of 1314 indicates a terminus for Riccobaldo's manuscript.[4] Thus a mention of an artist and his work, especially the famous Giotto, is not inappropriate to the tenor of the *Compilatio.*

The reliability of the Riccobaldo passage has gained support from the discovery of a record of Giotto's presence in Assisi. The document, of which we have a fragment in Bevagna, is the *Protocoll of Giovanni Alberti* for the years 1307–17.[5] The sense is that Giotto di Bondone of Florence and a painter named Palmerino di Guido had borrowed a sum of money in Assisi, and now, on January 4, 1309, Palmerino is repaying the debt in behalf of himself and (the absent) Giotto. One may suppose that Palmerino was a local painter of Assisi or thereabouts, with whom the visiting Florentine master quite logically dealt as today an architect working in another city would join forces with a firm that knew the local rules and usages. The loan may have been for supplies and wages paid in advance; by the beginning of 1309, Giotto received payment for the work and the debt could be retired. One supposes the document must refer to some painting probably carried out in 1308.

In all likelihood, the project was the decoration of the Magdalen Chapel in the lower church at Assisi. These frescoes are closer to the master than anything else in Assisi and are the earliest works there by Giotto's shop, as well as the only ones where we feel a limited, direct intervention of the master himself. The style of such a fresco as the Resurrection scene commonly called the *Noli Me Tangere* (Fig. 71) bears this out; it is so close to Padua that the assistant or assistants who carried out the large part of the program must have been intimately familiar with and recently involved in Giotto's shop during the first decade of the fourteenth century. It appears as though they also had considerable leeway with the designs that Giotto may have provided: the arrangement of the figures in their settings misses the perfection of those for the same scenes in the Arena Chapel, as Borsook has pointed out.[6]

Giotto, perhaps as part of the contractual agreement, appears to have painted one section, that with the donor Tebaldo Pontano kneeling before the

Magdalen.[7] This unusual image of the Mary Magdalen—a robust figure, swaying in gentle contrapposto, exuding matronly warmth—was conceived, I believe, under the spell of Giovanni Pisano, whose *Madonna* in the Arena Chapel was well known to Giotto. That it has the authority of a Giotto concept and is of the highest quality is attested in a comparison with the other portrait of the donor in the same chapel, Bishop Pontano with S. Rufino, which is clearly the work of an assistant.

We have gone into the question of the Magdalen Chapel in such detail because of the likelihood that it was this very impressive ensemble that Riccobaldo was signaling in his *Compilatio,* and not, as so many have assumed, the Legend in the upper church. Thus the famous *Chronicle* is scarcely any help in the dating of the St. Francis cycle in the upper church.

More than a century later, Lorenzo Ghiberti, in a much-discussed passage of his *Commentari,* wrote of Giotto having painted in Assisi, specifying that he had done "quasi tutta la parte di sotto (almost all of the part below)."[8] This has been interpreted to mean the frescoes below the biblical series on the walls of the upper church, in other words, the frescoes of the St. Francis Legend. In effect, then, Ghiberti attributed almost all of the Legend to Giotto. Of course, *sotto* can also be rendered as below or underneath, referring to the lower church, and it has occasionally been suggested that Ghiberti had the lower church in mind in his elliptical phrase. Indeed, to go around the lower church is to gain an impression that it is decorated very largely in a Giottesque mode: the impressive crossing vaults, the right transept, the St. Nicholas Chapel, and the Magdalen Chapel.

If Peter Murray was correct in his recent assessment of the *Commentari,* the word *parte* may be an error of transcription.[9] Ghiberti may have written the word *parete,* or *pariete,* meaning "wall" in the lost holograph original—an error of transcription that occurred elsewhere in the same epoch, as Murray demonstrated. In that case, "almost all of the [wall] below" would surely refer to the St. Francis Legend. When all this has been said, we are not much farther along, considering Ghiberti's likely margin for error and our quite reasonable reluctance to accept his word for Giotto's participation in the St. Francis cycle.[10] Thus, no early sources can assure us either of Giotto's authorship of the frescoes or, consequently, of that early date critics have insisted on to justify their attribution to Giotto.

It has sometimes been proposed that the frescoes must predate the final enlargement of the Torre del Popolo, which rises between the Palazzo del Capitano del Popolo (also called the Palazzo del Podestà) and the church of Santa Maria sopra Minerva in the central piazza of Assisi (Fig. 73). Years ago, P. Leone

73. (Top) Torre del Popolo and Temple of Minerva, Assisi

74. (Bottom) *Pietro Bernardone Arriving at San Damiano,* San Damiano (near Assisi)

Bracaloni asserted that this tower was shown in an unfinished state in the first scene of the Legend, *St. Francis Honored by a Simple Man* (Fig. 1).[11] His proof was to be found in what he thought was a Giottesque fresco (Fig. 74) of circa 1305–15 in the little church of San Damiano just outside Assisi. In the fresco, a club-wielding Pietro Bernardone menaces his son, Francis, while behind him we see Assisi rising on its hill. Although it is true that the tower in the fresco has crenellations like those on the actual tower and that these are absent from the tower in the St. Francis Legend, the matter is academic. This not very accomplished fresco in San Damiano is deeply in debt to the work of Ambrogio Lorenzetti, and one would hesitate to date it before the middle of the 1330s or later.[12] As such, the San Damiano fresco scarcely offers proof of an early date for the fresco in the upper church. Bracaloni might well have checked his theory against the elaborately delicate Gothic windows of the Palazzo del Capitano del Popolo in the *St. Francis Honored by a Simple Man,* surely evidence of the lateness of the fresco.

Among the other theories promulgated in defense of an early date for the Legend is that Giotto went to Rome in connection with the Jubilee of 1300, so that the Assisi frescoes had to have been finished before he left.[13] A much-repainted fragment of a once larger fresco in the Lateran, said to show Pope Boniface VIII blessing the populace, probably in the course of promulgating the Jubilee of 1300, has very often been accepted as a work by Giotto. On the other hand, as Charles Mitchell has demonstrated, the mention of Giotto's name in connection with the Lateran fresco dates back only to the seventeenth century.[14] That it has nothing to do with Giotto, and certainly cannot be offered as proof of his being in the city of Rome in 1300, is clear from the fragment. This is enforced by a glance at the entire fresco as it is preserved in a seventeenth-century drawing (Fig. 75) in the Ambrogian Library, Milan, in which we see an advanced naturalism of a later decade. The argument that the Assisi Legend had to have been completed before 1300 on the presumption that it had been executed by Giotto and that Giotto had left by 1300 is implausible.

More recently, Luigi Bellosi has proposed an even earlier date for the cycle at Assisi: 1288–92, during the papacy of Nicholas IV.[15] According to Bellosi, the representation of a beardless St. Francis was not only popular during the early fourteenth century but made for a more suitable image of the saint at the time of the Spiritualist controversy. Not until Taddeo Gaddi and the 1330s, says the author, did the beard return to fashion. Among his examples of the beardless St. Francis are Giotto's images in the Bardi Chapel of Santa Croce, Torriti's mosaic in the apse of Santa Maria Maggiore of 1296, and the image of

75. *Boniface VIII Proclaiming the 1300 Jubilee,* Sketch, Ambrosian Library, Milan

the saint in Cavallini's fresco on the monument of Cardinal Acquasparta (died 1302) in Santa Maria in Aracoeli. But the evidence for this theory is not sufficient to be decisive in defense of a pre-1290 date for the St. Francis cycle. In fact, it could as well be used in defense of a date after the return of the beard to fashion in the 1330s.

Of all the supposed proofs put forward from time to time in defense of a relatively early *terminus post quem* for the cycle in Assisi, none has had such universal approbation as the 1307 date on the altarpiece (Fig. 76) in the Gardner Museum, Boston, signed by Giuliano da Rimini.[16] We are not so sure that such important matters concerning Trecento painting should be decided on the basis of this date, which may, as it turns out, be problematical. In any case, it has been proposed that the St. Francis figure (Fig. 77) derives from that in the *Stigmatization of St. Francis,* scene XIX (Fig. 19), in the upper church: the saint kneels on his right knee and gazes up at the Seraphic Christ, from whom issue the stigmata. The first to signal this similarity was John White;[17] he was followed by Millard Meiss, who also thought that Giuliano imitated the *St. Clare* (Fig. 114) in the St. Nicholas Chapel of the lower church on the same altarpiece.[18] Giuliano's dependence on Assisi then became a general, accepted part of the literature, so that eventually the date of 1307 could be used as a terminus for the St. Francis

76. (Above) Giuliano da Rimini, Altarpiece, Isabella Stewart Gardner Museum, Boston

77. (Left) *Stigmatization of St. Francis,* Detail of Fig. 76

cycle even without explanation or referral to the sources. It might be added that the kneeling Magdalen in her chapel in the lower church appears also to have been the source for the Magdalen on Giuliano's altarpiece. Meiss justifiably believed Giuliano had made drawings of various frescoes in Assisi and used these formulas later in his own work.

The inscription on the Gardner Museum altarpiece on which scholars have relied so heavily is highly informative. It tells us that Giuliano was of the Riminese school and that the painting was done in the time of Pope Clement V (1305–1314):

ANNO. DNI. MILLO. CCC. SETTIMO. IULIANUS. PICTOR. DE. ARIMINO. FECIT. OCHO.
PUS. TENPORE. DNI. CLEMENTIS. PP. QUINTO.

This would seem to be reliable information inasmuch as the altarpiece dated 1308 in nearby Cesi is also ascribed to the time of Clement V:

NOIE. DNI. AMEN. ANNO. DOMINI. MILLO. CCCVIII. CLEMENTIS. PP. V. INDICTIONE.
DNA. ELENA. FECIT. FIERI. HOC. OPUS.[19]

On the other hand, it is surprising to discover a similar legend in the inscription on the altarpiece (Fig. 78) by Baronzio in the Urbino Gallery:

ANNO. DNI. MILLO. CCCXL. QTO. TPE. DNI. CLEMATIS. PP. OC. OPUS. FECIT. IONNES.
BARONTIUS. DE. ARIMINO.[20]

This work is usually dated 1345, but the QTO (QUINTO) must refer not to the date but to Pope Clement V. Thus the date of the altarpiece should be read as 1340. Inasmuch as Clement V was long dead, the inscription on the Urbino panel is implausible. For whatever reason of cult or politics, the Urbino panel received an inscription recalling a long-dead pope, which may have been done at a time unrelated to the period the picture was painted.

It is a matter of some interest that Andrea da Firenze probably depicted Pope Clement V in the Spanish Chapel between 1366 and 1368 in the grandiose fresco of *Christian Learning,* often called the *Apotheosis of St. Thomas Aquinas.* Clement is the second figure from the left in the front row (Fig. 79), associated with the allegorical representation of *Canon Law,* and he is the only pope in the group of fourteen historical figures.[21] While it is true that Clement V was pope at Avignon, and was the first such, and that he never set foot in Italy during his papacy, he may have been held in esteem for a long time, even in Italy. For one thing, his approach to the Spirituals' controversy in his 1312 bull, *Exivi de paradiso,* was one of the most conciliatory of the period. For another, he founded the University of Perugia in 1307.

78. (Above) Giovanni Baronzio, Altarpiece, Galleria Nazionale delle Marche, Urbino

79. (Left) Andrea da Firenze, *Christian Learning,* Detail of Clement V, Spanish Chapel, Santa Maria Novella, Florence

The inscription on the Giuliano painting runs across the top of the panel and is matched with another across the bottom. These two bands have white letters painted on a black ground. There is also a third band, however, that runs across the middle. This one is in sgraffito, that is, the gold ground was covered with a band of blue and then the letters were scratched out to yield the names of the saints in the upper row. The luminous beauty of this inscription (now much darkened) makes one suspicious about the other inscription with the 1307 date: it is so difficult to imagine an artist using two different types of inscription on one panel painting that we must suppose the black band with white letters is a later change or substitution, or a restoration with revisions. Laboratory tests reveal this to be a problematic area in the picture.[22] If, though, like the Baronzio painting of 1340, this was some sort of commemorative inscription, then the name of the pope and the date have no relevance to the picture itself any more than the 1221 date had anything to do with the great *Madonna* in the Palazzo Pubblico of Siena, which Guido da Siena painted many years later than its inscription states.[23]

Critics have always been perplexed by the odd occurrence of a well-formed Riminese painting some time before that school began to flourish in any significant way. Bonicotti exclaimed that Giuliano was an almost isolated phenomenon;[24] Zeri wrote of the "serious lacuna between this work and the rest of Riminese painting, a lacuna that weighs heavily on the entire school."[25] Van Marle was, as so often, bewildered: if Giuliano's activity falls in the first quarter of the century, how does it happen that he so resembles the midcentury painter Baronzio?[26] As a matter of fact, our two documents concerning Giuliano are both later in time. In one of them, Giuliano's wife was spoken of as a widow in 1346.[27] The other document associates him with Pietro da Rimini in the making of the altarpiece, long since lost, for the Eremitani, Padua, in 1324.[28] Was he not the painter who worked with his old-time partner, Pietro da Rimini, on the frescoes in the St. Nicholas Chapel in the cathedral of Tolentino? These important frescoes have sometimes been dated around the middle of the century; Volpe believed them to be from between 1335 and 1348.[29] Those on the lower walls have nothing to do with that typically expressionistic and dramatic mode in the vaults that identifies the latter as the work of Pietro, but are instead in the hard, linear, and brightly colored style of the Gardner panel. In the *Child Nicholas Listens to an Augustinian Preach* (Fig. 80) we rediscover that neat, somewhat dry figure style, those white complexions accentuated by dark pupils of the eyes, and the slightly stiff posture and head turnings always typical of Giuliano.

From the literature we detect a scarcely concealed bafflement that a single,

80. (Above) *Child Nicholas Listens to an Augustinian Preach,* St. Nicholas Chapel, Cathedral, Tolentino

81. (Left) Vertine Master, *Madonna of the Misericordia,* San Bartolommeo, Vertine in Chianti

impressive picture of the Riminese school—that in the Gardner Museum—should have been created several decades before anything comparable appeared. But, of course, the picture had not been scrutinized as carefully as was warranted. When it was described, it was to point to elements that could corroborate the strangely early date, elements that we consider archaisms. We might more profitably look at the small figures kneeling to either side of the Madonna and Child. These appear to have been borrowed from the image of the Madonna of Mercy, also called the Misericordia.[30] It would be difficult to point to a representation of the Misericordia before about 1330, a time when it seems to emerge in a number of places. For example, there is one at Orvieto attributed to the St. Thomas Master, another at Santa Maria inter Angelos, Spoleto, usually dated earlier, and another (Fig. 81) at Vertine in Chianti by a follower of Duccio.[31] The fact that the artist took only the arrangement of these eight figures—five of them Poor Clares, one crowned woman, and two other secular women—but not the standing Madonna from the Misericordia theme has disguised his borrowing from the motif.

A study of the varied and rich fabric designs in the Gardner picture demonstrates their similarity to those sophisticated examples of the Riminese school of the 1320s and 1330s. These are all discussed in Brigitte Klesse's complete volume on fourteenth-century Italian silk stuffs, in which, however, many of her examples of Giotto's patterns are taken from the Assisi pictures—hardly a trustworthy approach to Giotto's fabric designs.[32]

No doubt Giuliano was in Assisi and he probably did, as Meiss suggested, make drawings of the things he saw. He would have admired the 1308 frescoes by Giotto and his shop in the Magdalen Chapel, the vivacious Franciscan Legend of the upper church, and the frescoes in the St. Nicholas Chapel that had probably only recently been completed. If, then, Giuliano is a painter well within the expectable parameters of the Riminese school of the second quarter of the fourteenth century, and if the date on the Boston altarpiece is a later accretion, the 1307 date on it can have no significance for the St. Francis cycle.[33]

From all of the foregoing, it may be suggested that the St. Francis cycle at Assisi is not, among other things, demonstrably proven to relate to the Generalship of Giovanni di Muro (1296–1305) by any discernible internal evidence. Nor can it be certainly demonstrated that the *Compilatio* of Riccobaldo Ferrarese is speaking precisely of the St. Francis cycle, as opposed, say, to the Magdalen frescoes in the lower church. As for Ghiberti's *Commentari*, one is free to associate his remarks on Giotto's work at Assisi with the St. Francis cycle, but there is no reliable evidence to corroborate his attribution of the frescoes to Giotto; at the same time, if he did indeed write "parte" and not "parete," his reference could as well have referred to decorations in the lower church.

Vasari's dating of the Legend and his attribution of it to Giotto were based on hearsay and what he had read. It would be unwise to rely too heavily upon him in so controversial a matter. As for the supposition that the Torre del Popolo in scene I proves an early date because a fresco in San Damiano shows the tower after it had been finished, it can only be said that the San Damiano fresco is considerably later than had been imagined, and that the tower in that scene as well as the one in the St. Francis cycle have the same stories and elements as does the tower we see today, altered only by artistic perceptions. That the Assisi frescoes date earlier than 1300 can scarcely be demonstrated by the Jubilee fresco in the Lateran, even if it could be proven that this were a work by Giotto. As for the bearding of St. Francis, it must be said that even if it were unfashionable to have a beard during the early years of the fourteenth century, one would be surprised not to find the saint bearded in his church at Assisi where, no matter how convivial the episodes of the narration, the imagery of the saint is consistently iconic. And, in any case, beards were in full favor in the period at which it would appear that the Legend was painted, as we demonstrate elsewhere. Finally, the 1307 date on the picture by Giuliano da Rimini in the Gardner Museum is not beyond suspicion. Here again it would be unwise to rely too heavily upon it in the controversial dating of the Franciscan cycle at Assisi.

If, then, so many ties that seemed to bind the St. Francis cycle to an early date and to Giotto in a formative stage are loosed, the cycle is, so to speak, set free to float toward its own natural mooring—a mooring determined by numberless signals that issue from the pictures themselves.

NOTES

1. G. Vasari, *Le vite de' più eccellenti pittori, scultori ed architettori, scritte da Giorgio Vasari pittore aretino (1568),* ed. G. Milanesi, Florence, 1878, I, 377.

2. First published in Muratori, *Rerum italicarum scriptores,* Milan (25 vols. in 9, 1723–51), 1726, IX, col. 255. For a reproduction of the relevant part of the manuscript page, see B. Kleinschmidt, *Die Basilika San Francesco in Assisi,* 3 vols., Berlin, 1915–28, II, fig. 113. The author discusses the issue on pp. 155–56. See also P. Murray, "Notes on Some Early Giotto Sources," *Warburg Journal,* XVI, 1953, 58–80, especially 58–61. The suggestion of an interpolation was first made in 1912 by F. Rintelen, *Giotto und die Giotto-Apokryphen,* 2nd ed., Basel, 1912, 153. For a rejection of the interpolation theory, see C. Gnudi, "Il passo di Riccobaldo ferrarese relativo a Giotto e il problema della sua autenticità," in *Studies in the History of Art Dedicated to William E. Suida on His Eightieth Birthday,* London, 1959, 26–30, and his review of the matter in *Giotto,* Milan, 1959, 252–53.

P. L. Rambaldi also defended the authenticity of the passage in "Postilla al passo di Riccobaldo," *Rivista d'arte,* XIX, 1937, 349–56.

3. Murray, "Some Early Giotto Sources," 61.

4. Rintelen's belief that Riccobaldo's mention of Giotto might be an interpolation of a later time was based on the fact that the earliest extant manuscript of the *Compilatio* dates to the end of the fourteenth century (*Giotto-Apokryphen,* 152–53). The theory gained some adherents, especially since the verb used to describe Giotto's activity is "fuerit," normally used for the deceased. Of course, if the passage is an interpolation, it is irrelevant to the earliest literature.

5. V. Martinelli, "Un documento per Giotto ad Assisi," *Storia dell'arte,* XIX, 1973, 193–208; C. Censi, *Documentazione di vita assisiana, 1300–1448,* Grottaferrata, 1974, 51.

6. E. Borsook, *The Mural Painters of Tuscany,* 2nd ed., Oxford and New York, 1980, 16. See, for example, her analysis of the composition of the *Raising of Lazarus.* Borsook found four Giotto assistants at work in the Magdalen Chapel, including one who, she believed, painted the *Magdalen with Bishop Pontano.*

7. Bishop of Assisi, 1296–1329.

8. J. Schlosser, *Lorenzo Ghibertis Denkwürdigkeiten,* Berlin, 1912, 36; *I commentari,* ed. O. Morisani, Naples, 1947, 33.

9. P. Murray, "Ghiberti e il suo secondo Commentario," in *Lorenzo Ghiberti nel suo tempo. Atti del convegno internazionale di studi; Firenze, 18–21 ottobre, 1978,* II, Florence, 1980, 287.

10. A. Smart, in *The Assisi Problem and the Art of Giotto,* Oxford, 1971, 56, cites Ghiberti's attribution to Giotto of the frescoes in four Santa Croce chapels.

11. L. Bracaloni, "Assisi medioevale: studio storico-topografico," *Archivum franciscanum historicum,* VII, 1909, 3–19.

12. R. van Marle, *The Development of the Italian Schools of Painting,* V, The Hague, 1925, 65.

13. A. Venturi, *Storia dell'arte italiana* V, Milan, 1907, 290. The theory was still put forth almost as fact by E. Baccheschi in *The Complete Paintings of Giotto,* New York [ca. 1966], 90.

14. C. Mitchell, "The Lateran Fresco of Boniface VIII," *Journal of the Warburg and Courtauld Institutes,* XIV, 1951, 1–6; see also Smart (*Assisi Problem,* 108) for a brief account. Previtali gave the Jubilee fresco

to one of Giotto's "Roman assistants": *Giotto e la sua bottega,* Milan, 1967, 369.

15. L. Bellosi, "La barba di S. Francesco (nuove proposte per il problema di Assisi)," *Prospettiva,* 1980, no. 22, 11–34. Bellosi also concerned himself with the costumes in the Assisi cycle, finding them close in details to those in the 1283 dossal in Santa Chiara. But even though some points are acceptable, the time relationship between the 1283 panel and the fresco cycle is to be decided by weightier matters.

16. P. Hendy, *European and American Paintings in the Isabella Stewart Gardner Museum,* Boston, 1974, 110–12; this is a good account and includes a brief biography of the artist, a bibliography, and full quotation of inscriptions. See also C. Volpe, *La pittura riminese del Trecento,* Milan, 1965, 10–12, 69 (catalogue no. 1). My own opinions have been presented in "An Altarpiece by Giuliano da Rimini," *Fenway Court* (Gardner Museum publication), 1982, 14–27.

17. J. White, "The Date of the 'St. Francis Legend' at Assisi," *Burlington Magazine,* XCVIII, 1956, 344–51.

18. M. Meiss, *Giotto and Assisi,* New York, 1960, 3, 4. The St. Clare figure and therefore also her gestures are reversed in the Gardner picture.

19. Meiss supposed that the Cesi Master copied the *Madonna* on the rood screen in the *Verification of the Stigmata,* scene XXII, for the central image of his 1308 altarpiece in the cathedral at Cesi (*Giotto and Assisi,* 3–4). See also the same author's "Reflections of Assisi: A Tabernacle and the Cesi Master," *Scritti di storia dell'arte in onore di Mario Salmi,* II, Rome, 1962, 104–106.

20. Volpe, *Pittura riminese,* 86 (catalogue no. 76). For other comments on Baronzio, see the *Mostra della pittura riminese del Trecento, catalogo,* ed. C. Brandi, Rimini, 1935, xxii, 88ff., cat. no. 34 on 92–93.

21. A good many critics have agreed with this identification: G. Vasari, *Le vite,* 582; J. Wood-Brown, *The Dominican Church of Santa Maria Novella at Florence, a Historical, Architectural and Artistic Study,* Edinburgh, 1902, 166; A. Gotti, *Del trionfo di San Tommaso d'Aquino dipinta nel cappellone degli Spagnoli nel antico capitolo de' frati di Santa Maria Novella a Firenze,* Florence, 1887, 34; *New Catholic Encyclopedia,* III, New York, 1967, 929; see also F. Kenner, "Die Porträtsammlung des Erzherzogs Fer-

dinand von Tirol," *Jahrbuch der kunsthistorischen Sammlungen des allerhöchsten Kaiserhauses,* XVII, 1896, 101–274, esp. 121–22. The identification is not universally agreed to. J. von Schlosser wavers between Innocent IV and Gregory IX ("Giusto's Fresken in Padua und die Vorlaufer der Stanza della Segnatura," *Jahrbuch der kunsthistorischen Sammlungen des allerhöchsten Kaiserhauses,* XVII, 1896, 13–100, esp. 44–52). It has to be admitted that the emphatic fleur-de-lis pattern on his triple tiara would encourage one to believe the pope represented was French.

22. Although the testing at the laboratory of the Museum of Fine Arts, Boston, has not been completed, it has been confirmed that the white letters in the areas tested are later.

23. J. Stubblebine, *Guido da Siena,* Princeton, 1964, 30–41.

24. M. Bonicatti, *Trecentisti riminese: sulla formazione della pittura riminese del '300,* Rome, 1963, 34.

25. F. Zeri, "Una 'Deposizione' di scuola riminese," *Paragone,* no. 99, 1958, 50.

26. Van Marle, *Italian Schools,* IV, 1924, 316, 328.

27. L. Tonini, "Di Bitonto e della sua tavola di S. Giuliano non che di alcuni pittori che furono in Rimini," *Atti della deputazione di storia patria per la provincia di Romagna,* 1864, 7–8.

28. A. Moschetti, *Bollettino del Museo Civico di Padova,* 1931, 201; Zeri, "Una 'Deposizione,' " 48.

29. Volpe, *Pittura riminese,* 46, 85 (cat. no. 92), and numerous illustrations. Volpe dated the frescoes before 1348, the year the chapel was opened. Zeri (in "Una 'Deposizione,' " 50) did not dismiss Longhi's proposal (given in a lecture in Bologna, 1935) that Pietro's collaborator at Tolentino might have been Giuliano in a late phase. It is scarcely a coincidence that Pietro's signed *Crucifix* (Bonicatti, *Trecentisti riminese,* 73, fig. 73) still hangs in the Chiesa dei morti in the town of Urbania, near Urbino, the very same church for which Giuliano's Gardner picture had been painted.

30. The standard work is still V. Sussmann, "Maria mit dem Schutzmantel," *Marburger Jahrbuch für Kunstwissenschaft,* V, 1929, 285–351; see also P. Perdrizet, *La Vierge de Miséricorde; étude d'un thème iconographique,* Paris, 1908.

31. On the Orvieto panel formerly attributed to Lippo Memmi, see M. Mallory, "Thoughts Concerning the Master of the Glorification of St. Thomas," *Art Bulletin,* LVII, 1975, 12ff., fig. 12. On the Spoleto example, see van Marle, *Italian Schools,* IV, 408, and B. Rowland, Jr., "A Fresco Cycle from Spoleto," *Art in America,* XIX, 1931, 224–30, and fig. 4. On the Vertine panel, see J. Stubblebine, *Duccio di Buoninsegna and His School,* Princeton, 1979, I, 117–18; II, figs. 281–84. See also the *Misericordia* on fo. 1, ms. 52, in the Biblioteca Comunale, Bologna, dated 1329 (D. Fava, *Emilia e Romagna,* Milan, 1932, fig. 150). At this very time the theme is introduced into the triptych in Santa Chiara, Trieste, by Paolo Veneziano (R. Pallucchini, *La pittura veneziana del Trecento,* Venice, 1964, figs. 36 and 39).

32. B. Klesse, *Seidenstoffe in der italienischen Malerei des 14. Jahrhunderts,* Bern, 1967, 54, 133, cat. no. 91, fig. 180. The throne-back cloth in the Gardner picture has two overlapping design systems of plaited tendrils and quatrefoils, an arrangement Klesse found also on the apron pattern of the *Crucifix* in San Francesco, Rimini (ibid., 133, cat. no. 85a, fig. 179). This work, formerly considered to be by Giotto, is now more generally held to be a work of the Riminese school of the 1320s. A review of the literature can be found in Florence: Commissione della Mostra Giottesca, *Pittura italiana del Duecento e Trecento, catalogo della mostra giottesca di firenze del 1937,* eds. G. Sinibaldi and G. Brunetti, Florence, 1943, 581–83.

33. Despite his earlier belief that the St. Nicholas Chapel frescoes were later, Meiss was also constrained to date them before 1307 as a consequence of the similarity between the *St. Clare* there and the one on the Giuliano altarpiece (figs. 114 and 76).

V

The Actus Beati Francisci
and Other Legends Appearing
in the Early Fourteenth Century

Almost certainly the various written legends of St. Francis' life can be useful in determining the date of the Assisi fresco cycle. The ordering and dating of a number of these treatises has been the subject of extensive scholarly activity, as a result of which we have gradually evolved a fairly clear notion of when the various legends emerged.[1] The biographies came very early: Tommaso da Celano issued his *First Life,* or *Vita prima,* in 1230. To read this account is to experience St. Francis at close hand and to realize the compelling strength of his devotion to poverty and humility on the path that Christ had trod, all of which so electrified the thirteenth century.

Subsequent accounts increasingly distance us from the reality of the man, expunging as it were his reality in favor of his myth. Celano's account more nearly concentrated on the physical aspects, such as St. Francis' self-imposed poverty, which approached near squalor in his actual existence. Numerous references to his self-inflicted deprivations, especially of food, must account for the various illnesses that assailed him for so many years, especially the increasing blindness toward the end of his life, so that, in fact, many people were involved in keeping this frail creature alive.[2] It was in this context that the learned St. Bonaventure's more definitive and official *Major Legend,* or *Legenda major,* was issued in 1263, and we begin to see the outline of a more heroic saint. Both Celano and Bonaventure created second versions of their lives of St. Francis. Celano's is the *Second Life,* or *Vita seconda,* of 1244, while Bonaventure's is the *Minor Legend,* or *Legenda minor,* issued the same year as his *Major Legend,* that is, in 1263. There was a vast amount of other information about St. Francis during the thirteenth century, but we cannot be sure that it was all generally available. After all, with the issuance of Bonaventure's official interpretation, the directive went out that all other material should be destroyed. Fortunately, much of it seems merely to have been kept out of sight.

In the early fourteenth century use was made of a good deal of this material in several new legends that began to appear. One of these is the so-called *Legend of the Three Companions,* or *Legenda trium sociorum;* probably, the material was compiled by friars who had been close to St. Francis himself, Brothers Leo, Angelo, and Rufino. It may have been compiled as early as 1246, only to be "lost" until some time between 1320 and 1330, the period in the early fourteenth century that a manuscript based on this information first appeared. We know of some twenty manuscripts of this Legend. Another manuscript (ms. 1046 in the Perugia Library) that we call the Perugia manuscript is closely related to the *Trium sociorum* and it can be dated with fair certainty to 1311. It has been suggested that the unknown compiler relied on documents and other material made available to him in the Sacro Convento at Assisi.[3] Still another, more controversial Legend is the so-called *Mirror of Perfection,* or *Speculum perfectionis.* In the late nineteenth century Paul Sabatier published one of the many manuscripts of this legend—even then Sabatier knew of some forty-five copies.[4] More recently, it has been judged a sort of "literary forgery" of the early fourteenth century, probably produced around 1318.[5] Apparently, it was conceived as propaganda for the dissident and by then radicalized minority of the Spirituals, as the frequent references to St. Francis' actions and words about the life of poverty for the friars suggest. In any case, it would seem to have had its circulation chiefly amongst the dissident ranks of Spirituals. But even if it had not been that widely read, the Legend shares a number of characteristics with other early fourteenth-century versions.

It would be interesting to see in what ways these newly appearing manuscripts might be reflected in paintings of the time as, for example, in representations of that most conspicuous subject, the Stigmatization of St. Francis. In Guido da Siena's rendition of the theme (Fig. 82) in the latter part of the thirteenth century, the artist provided a wild, mountainous setting with caves and bears, and a cylindrical building, possibly a chapel, atop the hill. St. Francis in a kneeling position raises his arms straight up toward the angelic seraph hovering just above him. Although there are some variations in Stigmatizations of the thirteenth century, this might be taken as a typical example. When we turn to the one provided by Giotto just outside the Bardi Chapel in Santa Croce (Fig. 39), much of this earlier tradition continues. The mountainous mass behind the figure of the saint echoes the configuration of his kneeling form, as does the cave

set into the middle of the hill. To the right is a small chapel or oratory. Of course, everything is transformed by the powerful presentation of Giotto's heroic figure of St. Francis. This figure gains enormous spirituality from the extravagant contrapposto into which it is thrown, right knee raised, body swung round to the left and toward the image of Christ as seraph in the air above. The setting is stark and the mood is appropriately somber for so miraculous an occasion.

The conclusion is forced upon us that Giotto in the Bardi Chapel was following not only Bonaventure, as everyone did to some extent, but also the newer texts available to him by the 1320s when he executed the work. These all emphasize that St. Francis prayed solitudinously, away in the wildness of nature. This is clear in the wording of the Perugia manuscript (1311), where we learn that St. Francis "had no house or cell but took shelter under the rock of the mountain."[6] Similarly, in the *Speculum perfectionis* (1318), "He was not willing to have a well-built cell or house . . . but sheltered beneath the rocks in the mountains."[7] In the *Legend of the Three Companions* (1320–30) appeared the simplest description of all: "While praying on the side of a mountain called La Verna. . . ."[8] All these new texts depict an austerity in the Stigmatization, and Giotto's serene siting of his Bardi Chapel *Stigmatization* recalls vividly to us the new texts that would have been available to the artist in the 1320s.

There is another motif in one of the Bardi Chapel scenes that has always struck me as fairly indecipherable. One of Giotto's most exciting concepts in the chapel is the figure of St. Francis' father, Pietro Bernardone, in the *Renunciation of Worldly Goods* (Fig. 33): it is a study in ambivalence as the energetic contrapposto of his body suggests, while, at the same time, the curious expression on his face confirms a state of mental anguish. In the *Three Companions* (1320–30) we read that "His father rose up burning with grief and anger as he gathered up his garments and money and carried them home."[9] What a rare glimpse of an artist capturing in paint a literary image—words and brush of equal emotional potency.

In the same representation of the *Renunciation* (Fig. 30) one is struck by the youngsters, one to either side, with skirts held up to cradle what appear to be stones. Bonaventure is silent on the subject (Pietro Bernardone simply found the boy's inheritance money on a window sill). But when we read the literature contemporary to Giotto, all becomes clear. According to the *Legend of the Three Companions,* as St. Francis approached the bishop's palace, "townsfolk came out, insulted him, called him a fool and madman, and hurled stones and mud at him."[10] Obviously, for Giotto, this was an important element of the narrative and he used it to grand advantage. His youths take their places like corner figures on Greek pediments.[11]

We should not be surprised that painters of the early fourteenth century delighted in new scenarios as soon as they became available in literature; indeed, it would be incredible if they had not. Clearly, Giotto was interested in contemporary texts. And so too, I believe, were the Assisi artists. On the other hand, it quickly becomes apparent that at Assisi they had newer texts with which to play. To understand this, one more very significant Legend must be considered, the *Acts of St. Francis and His Companions,* or *Actus beati Francisci et sociorum eius,* written by the Marchigian friar Ugolino Boniscambi of Monte Santa Maria in the Marches (now Montegiorgio), sometime between the years 1327 and 1342. It would be safe to assume that this popular account went into circulation during the early 1330s. For his publication of this Legend in 1902, Sabatier consulted six manuscripts.[12]

To most scholars, the significance of the *Actus* lies in its use by a late fourteenth-century writer as a basis for his *I fioretti di San Francesco (The Little Flowers of St. Francis),* a compilation of a good number of the "chapters" from the *Actus* along with "Five Considerations on the Stigmatization," also based on the *Actus* but with highly dramatic extensions and elaborations.[13] In modern times, little attention has been paid to the *Actus* itself, which has, so to speak, been submerged within the vastly more popular *Fioretti.* For example, van Marle, in his *Development of the Italian Schools of Painting,*[14] is one of those who has spoken of the *Fioretti* as the source for certain elements in the Assisi *Stigmatization.* And indeed, we often enough encounter a less than clear distinction of the differences between the two texts—the *Actus* and the *Fioretti*—and of the time differential between them.

It is interesting to observe that in the invaluable *Omnibus* of Franciscan writings edited by Marion Habig, the *Actus* itself is not published, so that we are only presented with it as it is embedded in the *Fioretti* of the later fourteenth century. As we shall see, however, the *Actus* of the 1330s has some significance for our study. In the *Fioretti,* as some authors forget, much of the material was composed in the years between 1370 and 1385. If we were to compare the texts of the *Fioretti* and the *Actus* on the subject of the Stigmatization, bearing in mind what has been said of this episode in earlier texts, the development of the theme in a period of half a century becomes clear.

Of greatest importance here is the strikingly different tone in the description of the event of the Stigmatization. In the *Actus,* in chapters 4–27, we are told of the discovery of this quiet wilderness called Mount Alvernae.[15] In chapter 27, St. Francis and some brothers who were with him discover a poor peasant's hut there. The most important passage, however, comes in chapter 28, where "in a solitary place, cut off [*sequestratus*] from the others, St. Francis could pray, and he made a poor little hut [*pauperculam cellam*] on the side of the mountain. No one was to be allowed to come near, no one except Brother Leo." For most of the rest of the *Actus,* from chapters 29 to 70, we are given a personal account of Brother Leo's unabashed eavesdropping on St. Francis' prayers, on the saint's levitation from the ground, on the saint's conversations with the Lord, and on the strange incandescences that lit up the sky. Lastly, and with odd brevity, Leo explains how St. Francis confided to him the circumstances of the Stigmatization. We will pay no heed to the decorations added in the late fourteenth-century *Fioretti* (the courtesy call of Count Orlando, who had donated the land to St. Francis, or St. Francis' request that the count have a small structure built for him).[16] The original *Actus,* it appears, is to be understood almost as a first-hand account—tremulous, dramatic, personalized—by Brother Leo himself. And even though this material probably existed earlier, scholars have been unable to demonstrate its appearance in any known manuscript before the 1330s.

Although the Assisi cycle has been described as faithful to Bonaventure's account—especially because the inscription to each scene is quoted from his *Legenda major*—individual scenes may very well also have taken into consideration a later text, namely, the *Actus* which as we saw was probably in circulation only in the 1330s. In fact, it would be difficult to comprehend the *Stigmatization of St. Francis* (Fig. 19) in the Assisi cycle without such a precedent. At Assisi, instead of merely serving to echo the saint's figure, the mountain has also become the backdrop for an additional structure. Is it not, in fact, the "hut" or "cell" specified in chapter 28 of the *Actus,* the one that St. Francis built so that he could stay apart from the others and pray in solitude? In the course of all this, the Assisi artist was unable to hold onto that venerable part of the scenario to which we had grown so accustomed, the cave in the side of the mountain, which had still figured prominently in Giotto's fresco.

The most extraordinary aspect of the Assisi *Stigmatization* and one of the most unexpected iconographic details in the entire Assisi cycle is, of course, the presence of Brother Leo. He sits quietly in the lower right corner, his gaze turned down to the book in his hand. Is he reading, or lost in thought? Is it one of his ruses, pretending not to be aware of what St. Francis is doing? Or is he to be thought of as "entranced," as were Christ's disciples during the Transfiguration?[17] None of the legends claimed that Brother Leo was present at the Stigmatization, but the whole tenor of the 1330s *Actus* suggests him as the ideal "pseudo-witness" to the supernatural event.

The surprising fact remains that there is no instance prior to the representation of the *Stigmatization* at Assisi in which we have the accompanying figure of Brother Leo. His presence can only be explained by the scenario of the Stigmatization as it is set forth in the newly available *Actus*. Naturally, the motif is one of seductive charm; it adds narrative flavor to an otherwise uncompromisingly austere event. One is not surprised to find it quickly and frequently copied once the Assisi prototype came to artists' attention. It is noteworthy that other representations of the Stigmatization clearly echo the Assisi composition and most logically should be regarded as imitations of that popular and quite recent innovation. Of this we shall see more when we discuss the influence of the Assisi St. Francis cycle.[18]

A study of these St. Francis Legends emphasizes that an artist could be keenly appreciative of the new things being read at any particular time as variant texts made their appearance. What was in vogue when Giotto painted the Bardi Chapel in the 1320s was not the same thing that was in vogue in the 1330s when, apparently, the Assisi cycle was executed. It appears, then, that the Assisi masters were guided not only by the preceding Bardi Chapel narratives but by exciting elements of the Legend as set forth in the *Actus* and illustrated with particular clarity in the *Stigmatization*.

NOTES

1. M. Habig has edited a compendium of these: *St. Francis of Assisi: Writings and Early Biographies; English Omnibus of the Sources for the Life of St. Francis*, 3rd rev. ed., Chicago, 1973. For insights into the early legends, see also John V. Fleming, *From Bonaventure to Bellini, an Essay in Franciscan Exegesis*, Princeton, 1982.

2. A. Holl, *The Last Christian*, New York, 1980 (translated from the German: *Der letzte Christ*, 1979).

3. J. R. H. Moorman, "Early Franciscan Art and Literature," *Bulletin of the John Rylands Library*, Manchester, XXVII, 1942–43, 348.

4. P. Sabatier, *Le Speculum Perfectionis; ou, Mémoires de frère Léon*, Manchester, 1928; see also Alastair Smart, "The *Speculum Perfectionis* and Bellini's Frick St. Francis," *Apollo*, XCVII, 1973, 470–76.

5. Habig, *Omnibus*, 1109; Fleming, *Bonaventura to Bellini*, 16.

6. Habig, *Omnibus*, 990.

7. Ibid., 1134.

8. Ibid., 953.

9. Ibid., 909.

10. Ibid., 907.

11. The way in which the Assisi artists disguised this unseemly episode—one scarcely suitable for the saint's principal church—is in itself amusing, as we saw in Chapter II.

12. *Actus beati Francisci et sociorum eius*, ed. P. Sabatier, in *Collection d'études et de documents sur l'histoire religieuse et littéraire du moyen-âge*, IV, 1902. Andrew Little discovered another, more complete version of the *Actus* and published a comparative table of the differences between his manuscript and that published by Sabatier: "Description of a Franciscan Manuscript Formerly in the Phillips Library," *British Society of Franciscan Studies, Collectanae Franciscana*, V, 1914, 9–113. A long-lost version was

rediscovered in the Archivio di Stato, Siena (see B. Bughetti, "Una parziale nuova traduzione degli *Actus* accopiata ad alcuni capitoli dei Fioretti," *Archivum franciscanum historicum,* XXI, 1928, 515–52, and XXII, 1929, 63–113).

13. Habig, *Omnibus,* 1267–530.

14. R. van Marle, *The Development of the Italian Schools of Painting,* III, The Hague, 1924, 41.

15. The *Actus* is divided into seventy-one parts or "chapters," a number of which come to not much more than a sentence. See Sabatier, *Actus,* 31–39.

16. Habig, *Omnibus,* 1436.

17. I wish to thank Kavin Frederick for bringing this to my attention. See also Fleming, *Bonaventura to Bellini,* 92, 17.

18. These examples, discussed below in the chapter on the influence of the Assisi cycle, have the most varied origins, from Giotto's shop to the Neapolitan school.

VI

The Rise of Vernacular Art

Some two hundred years after the Legend of St. Francis in the upper church at Assisi had been painted, it could still evince the grandest encomium that Giorgio Vasari had to offer.[1] I cannot imagine that anyone ever appreciated these frescoes more than he—for the variety of the compositions, for the costumes of the period, for the arrangement, proportion, vivacity, and naturalness of the figures. It is true that Vasari very often preferred works of art in which an artist had managed crowds of figures skillfully and shown he had an eye for the variousness of things. For Vasari, multiplicity—well handled—was greater than simplicity, which was for him akin to poverty.

Almost certainly the original intention of the artists who worked on the St. Francis cycle was to achieve just those effects that Vasari praised. They were, no doubt, intentionally designed in a popular vein, purposefully employing a vernacular language of gesture, expression, costume, and architectural ambience. As Eugenio Battisti has stressed, the frescoes were meant for the crowds of pilgrims. Indeed, they were highly accessible in the wide, well-lit upper church, whereas Cimabue's apocalyptic scenes in the presbytery were pretty well hidden from the general public by the choir screen.[2]

There is every reason to believe that the St. Francis frescoes were intended to give visual evidence of the saint's miracles, and also to accrete visual symbols comparable to those long-established ones of early Christian saints. Not least, they were to emphasize the intimacy between the papacy and the Franciscan Order. Unquestionably, the surest way to effectuate these goals would be to illustrate the story in as broad a fashion as possible. Vasari's response to the frescoes differs hardly at all from the response of a pilgrim in the church today.

Thus Vasari's praise of the *Miracle of the Spring* (Fig. 14) appears to us to be naive; it is, however, an accurate gauge of his appreciation of these scenes and, as well, of the highly popular nature of the cycle. Vasari marveled to see the thirsty man lower himself to drink from the spring of water that St. Francis has miraculously caused to appear. For Vasari, it could be a real man there, really drinking. For Vasari, the figure is a celebration of life, and surely must have seemed so to the people of the fourteenth century. Stendhal, in the early nineteenth century—echoing, of course, Luigi Lanzi whom he had read assiduously —applauded the depiction of the man drinking at the spring.[3] Not even Raphael could have improved on it. What Vasari admired was, if we read him correctly, the verisimilitude of these Assisi narratives. This is achieved by all the various techniques available to an artist of realism.

In the fourteenth century the physical world swam into people's perceptions as it had never before, at least not since Roman times. When we read letters written by Petrarch, we feel closer to the flow of life; they reveal a man who was experiencing the phenomena of the real world much as we do, so that his letters have the freshness they would if they had been written by a friend but a few days ago. Especially is this so in the letter describing his climb of Mont Ventoux in the South of France during April 1336, which he did, he told us, for the curiosity of it. And for many this has marked Petrarch as a man of the modern world of individuality and experiental orientation. Along the way, as he and his brother labored up the slopes, an old man who had climbed the mountain fifty years before tried to dissuade them—he had gotten nothing but repentance and toil from it. One senses also that he felt a certain dread. After all, in the imagination of medieval folk, the fearsomeness and mystery of mountains arose in part because of their wildness but also in part because they were associated with sacred events: Moses on Mount Horeb, Christ transfigured on Mount Tabor, or St. Francis receiving the stigmata on Mount Alverna.

It is all there in Petrarch's letter: the physical discomfort, the fatique, and when he reached the summit, his being overwhelmed by the light, thin air and the spectacle of the view lying before him.[4] Petrarch opened a window on the world and in that sense illustrates in a most dramatic way the thrust of life and art as the fourteenth century went forward. Petrarch's experience gives us a glimpse of man in his environment just as the St. Francis Legend in Assisi does.

It was the Viennese art historian of the end of the last century, Max Dvořak, who helped us to see that fourteenth-century artists increasingly took sensual experience itself as subject matter.[5] They opened up to art the total range of the physical world and its inexhaustible multiplicity, so that their depictions were abundantly provided with the greatest possible number of natural observations of nature, and the content of their illustrations had richness and variety.

It is exactly this richness and variety, this realism of detail, that characterizes the cycle of paintings at Assisi. And it is these qualities that give the narratives their popular tone. Dvořak contrasted Giotto's very different mode—out of the raw material of experience he created a world of inner unity where the images are monumentalized; Dvořak's insightful characterization of Giotto is made, in part at least, to clarify the contrasting art of the realists.

Arnold Hauser, in his *Social History of Art*[6] describing the changes taking place in the late Middle Ages, saw the dynamic reality of the new images. The observation of detail was keen: furnishings of interiors, costumes, animals, even work tools became themselves the objects of artistic interest. In the pictures of the time, said Hauser, there was the "illusion of the journey." He speaks of the "travel landscape," with the spectator at the side of the road drawn into the illusion of life, entranced by the observations and descriptions. Hauser could have been describing the narratives on the walls of the upper church at Assisi.

In recent times, the critical appraisal of the narratives has not changed so very much. Cesare Gnudi (a firm believer in Giotto's authorship of the Assisi cycle) discerned in the frescoes a delight in description and narration and an insistence on detail of faces, costumes, and so forth.[7] For the first time in the history of painting, he wrote, an artist joyfully described life. In one figure, the nude St. Francis in the *Renunciation of Worldly Goods* (Fig. 5), Gnudi caught the "throb of life" [*fremito della vita*]. At the same time, he described the series as having—at least at the start—a "lofty serenity and solemn grandeur," phrases that may have to do with the author's belief in Giotto's authorship.

Robert Oertel could write that the frescoes "fascinate the most casual viewer with their intensity and forthright popular style."[8] He took note of the simple directness, as well as the bright and lively colors. The German critic believed that the Assisi cycle was the work of Giotto, and so, like Gnudi, he spoke also of the frescoes' "lofty monumentality and austere grandeur," almost the identical abstractions used by Gnudi.

In any discussion of Assisi, a critic will often enough put a finger on such factors as the secular approach, the realistic detail, or literary use of symbols. Eugenio Battisti, who also attributed the cycle at Assisi to Giotto, pointed out how different was our perception of these frescoes in comparison to Cimabue's Apocalypse scenes in the transepts with their "intimate religious fervor."[9] The St. Francis Legend, as Battisti rightly emphasized, treats of historical narrative and is increasingly secular in tone. Osvald Sirén illuminated our path, perhaps accidentally, during the course of listing his complaints against the Assisi frescoes when he stressed the artist's "remarkable interest in realistic detail" and his "decorative or literary talent."[10] And when John White analyzed the *Renunciation of Worldly Goods,* he spoke of the hand of God at the top of the scene as being "more of a literary symbol than a formal factor in the design."[11] Thus, in the long-lasting argument over whether or not Giotto participated in the Assisi cycle, critics of varying persuasions all share an underlying agreement that the cycle represents a new visual language, that of the vernacular. In such a mode of painting, a symbol can be inserted to aid in our reading of the story; and that was, after all, the principal aim of this series of narratives.

The two opinions by Gnudi and Oertel cited above lead one to the observation that while both critics comment with considerable perceptivity on the immediacy of the appeal of the frescoes, their convictions about the authorship force them to make statements about the grandeur and solemnity of the scenes, characterizations that are, to put it mildly, quite contrary to the idea of the popular art they are describing. And, in fact, one measure of the degree to which the artists at Assisi strove for this new, more popular approach for a wider audience is the degree to which they relentlessly drove out all vestiges of monumentality. Indeed, the cycle's "popular" quality derives from and is dependent on the very absence of monumentality, that is, the timeless, the abstracted, that which is outside of accidental causality. In the Assisi pictures, it is this accidental, often trivial and amusing detail that entrances the spectator into the illusion of their reality.

In his last will and testament, Petrarch in the course of bequeathing to a friend his picture of the Virgin by Giotto pauses to characterize the picture as being beyond the comprehension of the ignorant, but those who know art marvel at it.[12] It seems important to recognize that a perception we have in this century is not so very different from a perception that was had in the fourteenth century: art for the few is not the same as art for the multitude. Clearly, it was the obligation of the artists at work on the St. Francis cycle in the upper church at Assisi to instruct, explain, delight, and even amuse or do whatever else was necessary to inspire the common people. It is extraordinary that still today groups of people cluster in front of certain frescoes at Assisi, for example, the *Miracle of the Spring* (Fig. 14) or the *Sermon to the Birds* (Fig. 15), their faces filled with comprehension, and therefore with pleasure and wonderment.

Had it not been for the question of Giotto's participation, which has preoccupied so many scholars for so long a time, we would long since have had a keener appreciation of the nature of these paintings at Assisi. Raimond van Marle, who had a great deal of difficulty justifying to himself the attribution of the Assisi cycle to Giotto, is driven to say that "Giotto did not trouble much about his compositions and expression of dimensions, he wanted to tell his stories by means of living and acting figures," and again, "the artist always pays particular attention to the psychological importance of the moment, attempting most of all to produce truthful dramatic representations of the events in which the diversity of the human emotion is understood and rendered in a perfectly modern spirit."[13] Howsoever van Marle misstated the case for Giotto, he was perceiving more than he may have realized about the aims and achievements of the artists who created the Assisi St. Francis cycle.

In a description of Taddeo Gaddi's art written some years ago, Richard Offner noted that as Taddeo got away from Giotto's influence, "his manner drifted along with the age towards literary expressiveness." And he added that "the sense of seeing so strong in earlier artists was growing feebler than the sense of sentiment or situation."[14] This is the exact tenor of Oertel's remarks on Taddeo. He wrote of the artist's abandoning Giotto's idealized types and classical rhythms. In the Baroncelli Chapel in Santa Croce, Oertel saw animated crowds, even birds nesting in the foliage of trees, and a "remarkable naturalism in the rendering of supernatural light."[15] In the Baroncelli Chapel (which nowadays is dated to between 1328–35 instead of later),[16] our attention is divided between the spectacles of the *Adoration of the Shepherds*—so accomplished and early an example of radiant night light as a recognizable, experienced phenomenon—and the *Presentation of the Virgin in the Temple* (Fig. 83), with its pleasing, eye-catching details of architectural complexes, and of figures deployed inside and outside in ways that are, again, recognizable and experiential.

Such an art as we see practiced here by Taddeo Gaddi is, it must be admitted, in the vernacular language. Something of this voracious appetite for reality is to be found also in the narratives surrounding Taddeo's *Tree of Life* (Fig. 84), a fresco in the Santa Croce refectory, probably of the 1330s. In the episode of *St. Louis of Toulouse Serving the Poor* (Fig. 85), the attention is quickly taken by the costumes, the victuals on the table, the man quaffing his wine, the elaborations of interior and exterior space. The saint and his actions have ceased to be the sole point of interest; they are to be appreciated in their physical context.

The quotations from Offner and Oertel offered above are far from isolated in the literature. Commentary on Taddeo Gaddi has often emphasized this aspect of his work as a measure of his withdrawal from the more purely Giottesque modes. Surely, though, it may also be attributed to a major new tendency in art.

When we examine the art of one of Taddeo's elder contemporaries, Pacino di Bonaguida, who flourished in the first several decades of the fourteenth

83. (Top left) Taddeo Gaddi, *Presentation of the Virgin in the Temple,* Baroncelli Chapel, Santa Croce, Florence

84. (Above) Taddeo Gaddi, *Tree of Life,* Refectory, Santa Croce, Florence

85. (Right) *St. Louis of Toulouse Serving the Poor,* Detail of Fig. 84

century, the differences become clearer.[17] Pacino's *Tree of Life* panel (Fig. 86) of circa 1305 in the Florence Academy purveys no such detailed or anecdotal accounting.[18] Every non-essential object is excluded, interior spaces are given little definition, and even the seated hosts at the top of the panel are presented in a fashion not notably different from the tiered figures in the *Last Judgment* mosaic in the Florence Baptistery of the mid-thirteenth century. Likewise, the Passion narratives of his Pierpont Morgan manuscript (Fig. 87), of circa 1300, echo the figural and spatial modes of the Dugento, with the merest hint of Giotto's first impact on the Florentine school.[19] As Offner realized, Pacino emerged "out of the blind gap between the Dugento and the Trecento."[20] Nor can we say that these narratives in his *Tree of Life* and the Morgan manuscript are simplified because of the miniaturistic nature of the work. On the contrary, Taddeo's small narratives from the *armadio,* or cabinet, in the Florence Academy of the 1330s are full of complex architectural settings. As for these works by Pacino, it must be said that one could not find better exemplars, nor, therefore, better monitors of Florentine painting in the first years of the fourteenth century.

86. Pacino di Bonaguida, Detail of the *Tree of Life,* Galleria dell'Accademia, Florence

87. Pacino di Bonaguida, *Pentecost,* M643, Fo. 29, Pierpont Morgan Library, New York

If we seek an intermediary between Pacino and Taddeo, we might turn to Simone Martini and his frescoes (Fig. 88) in the St. Martin Chapel of the lower church at Assisi, the date of which is much discussed but which are widely agreed to belong to the 1320s.[21] There we are asked to note distinctions and varieties of costumes and fabrics, the details of rooms with their fenestrations and columns. Over everything is a quiet hum of activity and of communication, the sense of speech, and even of song. For density of detail and of space occupancy, it would be hard to find comparable examples in fourteenth-century Italian painting. One comes to the conclusion that French Gothic manuscript illuminations may already have been of interest to Simone. French influence would also go a long way to explain the unmistakable note of sophisticated wit that underlies these narratives.

Pietro Lorenzetti himself participated little in the move toward a more vernacular presentation until his 1342 *Birth of the Virgin,* which is a fulsome, oft-cited example of the new realism. On the other hand, his assistant, who worked on part of the cycle in the left transept of the lower church—as, for example, in the *Entry into Jerusalem* and the *Last Supper* (Fig. 89)—took advantage of the newer modes of narrative richness that were accumulating all around him at this time, surely not before the 1330s. The modern examination of the

88. Simone Martini, *Death and Ascension of St. Martin,* San Martino Chapel, Lower Church, Assisi

89. Pietro Lorenzetti Shop, *Last Supper,* Lower Church, Assisi

sequence in which the frescoes were executed suggests that the assistant painted the *Entry into Jerusalem* through the *Via Crucis* before Pietro began his grand *Crucifixion* and the austere scenes on the end wall from the *Descent into Limbo* through the *Resurrection.* Thus we see that Pietro at Assisi in the latter half of the 1330s achieved a new monumentality, while his assistant already belonged to the younger generation of reality-oriented artists.[22]

Ambrogio Lorenzetti's *Good Government* frescoes (Fig. 90) in the Siena Palazzo Pubblico must represent the apogee of the new realism. This celebration of life in the countryside and in the city, coming in the last two years or so of the 1330s, attests to a newly focused interest of both artist and audience that would have been inconceivable at an earlier point in fourteenth-century Italian art. It exhibits a veritable encyclopedia of mundane, sometimes trivial, and even amusing details of daily life, with the quite grandiose goal of celebrating life itself in the country and the city.

90. Ambrogio Lorenzetti, *Good Government in the City,* Detail, Palazzo Pubblico, Siena

NOTES

1. G. Vasari, *Le vite dé più eccellenti pittori, scultori ed architettori,* ed. G. Milanesi, I, Florence, 1878, 377–78; idem, eds. R. Bettini and P. Barocchi, II text, Florence, 1967, 100–101.

2. E. Battisti, *Giotto, Biographical and Critical Study,* Lausanne, 1960, 52–53.

3. M. H. Beyle (Stendhal), *Histoire de la peinture en Italie,* in *Oeuvres complètes de Stendhal,* III, Paris,

1953, ch. VIII, 53–54; L. Lanzi, *Storia pittorica dell'Italia dal risorgimento delle belle arti fin presso la fina del XVIII secolo,* 6 vols., Bolzano, 1789. For a connection between Lanzi and Stendhal, see D. Wakefield, *Stendhal and the Arts,* New York and London, 1973.

4. Petrarch, *Le familiari, libri I–IV,* ed. U. Dotti, Urbino, 1970, 482–501. See also E. R. Tatham, *Francesco Petrarca, the First Modern Man of Letters; His*

Life and Correspondence (1304–1347), 2 vols., London, 1925–26, ch. IX, 291–363.

5. M. Dvořak, *Idealism and Naturalism in Gothic Art,* Notre Dame, Indiana, 1967, 135ff. (Translated from *Idealismus und Naturalismus in der gotischen Sculptur und Malerei,* Munich, 1918.)

6. A. Hauser, *The Social History of Art,* I, New York, 1951, 263–64.

7. C. Gnudi, *Giotto,* Milan, 1959, 73–94.

8. R. Oertel, *Early Italian Painting to 1400,* London [ca. 1968] 64.

9. Battisti, *Giotto,* 53.

10. O. Sirén, *Giotto and Some of His Followers,* Cambridge (Mass.), London and Oxford, 1917, 19.

11. J. White, *Art and Architecture in Italy, 1250–1400,* Baltimore, 1966, 140.

12. F. Petrarch, *Petrarch's Testament,* trans. and ed. T. Mommsen, Ithaca, N.Y., 1957, 12.

13. R. van Marle, *The Development of the Italian Schools of Painting,* III, The Hague, 1924, 46–47.

14. R. Offner, "Two Unknown Paintings by Taddeo Gaddi," in *Studies in Florentine Painting, the Fourteenth Century,* New York, 1927, 60.

15. Oertel, *Early Italian Painting,* 189.

16. Oertel, ibid., and C. Isermeyer, *Rahmengliederung und Bildfolge in der Wandmalerei bei Giotto und den florentiner Malerei des 14. Jahrhunderts,* Würzburg, 1937, 488. On the other hand, in a recent, complete monograph on Taddeo, the chapel decoration is dated still earlier, circa 1328–30 (A. Ladis, *Taddeo Gaddi, Critical Reappraisals and Catalogue Raisonné,* Columbia, Mo., and London, 1982, 88–112).

17. The basic study of Pacino di Buonaguida is that of R. Offner, in his *A Critical and Historical Corpus of Florentine Painting,* sec. III, vol. II, part I, New York, 1930. He is documented as a painter for the first time in 1303 (ibid., 2). See also Smart, *The Assisi Problem and the Art of Giotto,* Oxford, 1971, 235–36.

18. For the dating of the panel, see Offner, *Corpus,* 8; for illustrations, plates II to II.[14]

19. Pierpont Morgan Library, ms. 643; Offner, ibid., plates VIII–VIII.[17]

20. Offner, ibid., 1.

21. G. Paccagnini, *Simone Martini,* Milan, 1957, 137 (Italian edition, 1955); idem, in *Encyclopedia of World Art,* New York, 1964, cols. 502, 506. See also M. Boskovits, "Celebrazioni dell' VIII Centenario della nascità di San Francesco, studi recenti sulla basilica di Assisi," *Arte cristiana,* n.s., LXXI, 1983, 214.

22. Robin Simon would have the St. Martin Chapel finished before 1317–19 insofar as it most likely preceded the work by Pietro Lorenzetti in the left transept ("Towards a Relative Chronology of the Frescoes in the Lower Church of St. Francis at Assisi," *Burlington Magazine,* CXVIII, 1976, 361–66. In this Simon is following, but hesitantly, the schedule laid out by Hayden Maginnis for Pietro's work ("Assisi Revisited: Notes on Recent Observations," *Burlington Magazine,* CXVII, 1975, 511–17, esp. 512, 515; "The Passion Cycle in the Lower Church of San Francesco, Assisi: The Technical Evidence," *Zeitschrift für Kunstgeschichte,* XXXIX, 1976, 193–208). Maginnis based his arguments on an examination with L. Tintori of the *giornate.*

VII

Vernacular Art, circa 1340

As we have seen in the preceding chapter, vernacular art was commonplace in Italian art by the beginning of the 1340s. We come to the conclusion that if the Simone Martini frescoes (Fig. 88) at Assisi represent an early stage of this development, the Ambrogio Lorenzetti frescoes (Fig. 90) in the Palazzo Pubblico of Siena represent the fullest statement of the movement. There are numerous examples by that time. We might begin with a look at the illustrations in the Biadaiolo *Codex,* a work that dates to just about 1340. Of this artist, Offner could say that he had "a racy prose idiom," and he quoted Bombe's remarks on the "popular" nature of his art.[1] Indeed, the Biadaiolo Master's images are highly secularized and witty, as we determine in, among others, his scene set in the Florence cornmarket (Fig. 91). This bustling activity and the inventory of objects in the picture have become the subject matter. Ambrogio's frescoed account of city life is exactly parallel.

Very probably three altarpieces, all usually dated considerably earlier, belong to this stage of the arts around 1340: the St. Cecilia and St. Humilitas panels (Figs. 96 and 94) in the Uffizi, and the St. Minias altarpiece (Fig. 92) in the church of San Miniato al Monte, Florence. The San Miniato panel is now generally agreed to be a major work by Jacopo del Casentino, who is documented in 1339 and 1347, and who was dead in 1358.[2] The conservative nature of his panel shapes and figure types, and his relationship to the St. Cecilia Master (presumed to be earlier), have prevented critics from judging this altarpiece as a work of such a late date. But as Luigi Dami has demonstrated, the chapel for which the panel was painted was renovated between 1335 and 1442, so that the panel was most probably made for installation at the latter date.[3] Jacopo's narratives are conceived in a zealously realistic fashion. No opportunity is missed to depict buildings of two stories and to squeeze figures into their balconies or, so

91. Biadaiolo Master, *Cornmarket of Florence,* Ms. Tempiano 3, Fo. 79, Laurentian Library, Florence

characteristic of the period, to create a lively narrative of a street scene, as in the *Taming of the Leopard Set Against St. Minias* (Fig. 93), or *St. Minias Tempted by Gold Plate*.[4] In such narratives as *St. Minias Set on a Gallows* and the *Decapitation of St. Minias,* one comprehends the gulf between Jacopo and that painter of the first decade of the century whom we discussed earlier, Pacino di Bonaguida.

Turning to the narratives on the Uffizi altarpiece of St. Humilitas (Fig. 95), we have a comparable experience of situational dramas replete with busy street scenes and carefully detailed interiors. That any of this could represent the hand or, indeed, the mind of Pietro Lorenzetti as some affirm is difficult to believe. And to date it to the year 1316—at a time when as some say Pietro would have been free to execute it—is equally incomprehensible. As it happens, the panel

92. Jacopo del Casenti
Minias and His Lege
Miniato al Monte, Fl

101

93. *Taming of the Leopard Set Against St. Minias,* Detail of Fig. 92

bears an inscription purportedly copied from a lost original, and critics have always been divided as to whether that original had a date of 1316 or 1341, that is, whether the numerals represented CCXVI or CCXLI.[5] As DeWald pointed out years ago, the architecture and the relationship of the figures to it is so advanced in these scenes that a 1316 date is highly improbable.[6] More recently, Luisa Marcucci has demonstrated how a number of iconographic factors urge a later date: Beata Margherita, who kneels beside the main figure, died in 1330, and in any case, the Legend of Beata Humilitas was only fixed in 1332.[7] Everything would indicate that the original inscription did indeed read 1341, and all the stylistic factors bear out such a reading.

The third of the three altarpieces in this group is the one in the Uffizi (Fig. 96) which gives the name to the artist, the St. Cecilia Master.[8] The narrative flavor of these little scenes fits very well with all the others where we found animated figures briskly acting out lively events against elaborate architectural concoctions. The contemporaneity of this altarpiece to the one discussed above by Jacopo del Casentino is demonstrable in many ways, but perhaps especially in the settings, as in a comparison between the *St. Cecilia Preaching Before Valerian*

94. (Above) *St. Humilitas and Her Legend,* Uffizi, Florence

95. (Right) *St. Humilitas Reading During Supper,* Detail of Fig. 94

96. (Above) St. Cecilia Master, *St. Cecilia and Her Legend,* Uffizi, Florence

97. (Left) *St. Cecilia Preaching Before Valerian and Tiburtius,* Detail of Fig. 96

and Tiburtius (Fig. 97) and Jacopo's *Taming of the Leopard Set Against St. Minias.* Both contain tall, slender architecture that could have been, one imagines, fabricated by the same artist. The compositional ideas are the same in both, having the same high ground-floor rooms and small attic rooms or loggias. The petite scale of the figures in relation both to the architecture and to the height of the scene is also nearly identical. That they are by different artists can be shown in the St. Cecilia Master's more mannered figures and in his architectural parts, seemingly cast in a mold and recombined in endless variety, uniformly lit on the front and darkly shadowed in the openings. But the two artists were surely contemporaries, who knew each other's style intimately.

The dating of this Uffizi altarpiece is, of course, the most controversial of all inasmuch as a great deal of early Trecento art has been seen in direct relation to its date. The chronology of the St. Cecilia Master has been misconstrued, chiefly I suppose from the perceived necessity of placing his Assisi frescoes (Figs. 1, 26, 27, and 28) early in his career. If it were not for his participation in the St. Francis cycle at Assisi—presumably around 1300, according to most authorities—we might have developed a very different career span for this artist. A careful study of his *St. Margaret* altarpiece (Fig. 98) in Santa Margherita a Montici should have persuaded us that this altarpiece represented his early style:[9] the poetic pantomime of the figures, and a lyrical miniaturistic style, both qualities similar to Pacino's delicate little scenes (Fig. 87). The simple, cardboard-like settings subtly binding the compositions have as yet none of the fantastic quality they will assume in his later St. Cecilia altarpiece. Finally, the whole is set into a low-slung gable shape very close to thirteenth-century prototypes.

We must conclude, as others have, that the 1307 *St. Peter* in Santi Simone e Giuda, Florence, is not a work by this master.[10] Although the picture has been considered to be a collaborative work, or from the shop of the St. Cecilia Master, it should probably be eliminated entirely from his oeuvre. In any case, it seems unwise to use its 1307 date as one of the guides to the St. Cecilia Master's work at Assisi, and therefore to the dating of the cycle, as Smart did. Very unlike the *St. Peter* is the delicate *Madonna and Saints* in Santa Margherita a Montici, a work of the same early period as his *St. Margaret* in the same church.[11] The San Giorgio alla Costa *Madonna,* originally considered by Offner to be from the hand of the St. Cecilia Master, was in a second moment removed by Offner from the list of attributions to him and reattributed to the painter of the Santa Maria Novella *Crucifix.*[12] Between his opinion and that of many other critics who have insisted that both were works by Giotto himself,[13] we are increasingly aware that the

98. St. Cecilia Master, *St. Margaret and Her Legend,* Santa Margherita a Montici, Florence

Madonna should not remain among the works attributed to the St. Cecilia Master. Indeed, eliminating these large pictures from the master's creations improves the sense of orderly relationship between the various works that are his.

If the St. Margaret altarpiece is perceived as an early expression of the genius of the St. Cecilia Master, it must also be perceived that the Uffizi altarpiece shows an absorption with elaborate stage sets, a sophisticated control of figures set into his spaces, and a mannered, hardened style very unlikely for a young artist. Logically, we should have thought of the St. Cecilia panel as a later, less delicately conceived work. One has, of course, been quite right to relate the style of the St. Cecilia picture to the frescoes this artist did in Assisi, where the quality of architectural fantasy is so similar, and where the extraordinary elongation of some of the figures as well as the artifice of their postures recalls his Uffizi altarpiece. One can only conclude that it is the date of the Assisi frescoes that has not been correctly understood.

Critics have had a certain date on which to rely in placing the St. Cecilia altarpiece; presumably, it has been thought, the panel was placed in the church of Santa Cecilia some time before it was destroyed by fire in 1304.[14] On the face of it, this is a dubious notion, and critics have consistently skirted speculation as to how the altarpiece escaped damage or destruction in the conflagration. But many years ago, Schubring and Suida demonstrated that the picture may just as well have been painted for the newly rebuilt church.[15] Inasmuch as the stylistic factors of the altarpiece dovetail very nicely with a later date, we must conclude that the altarpiece belongs, in fact, to a time some forty years after what is usually supposed. Of course, it does not stand alone: beside it are the 1341 Beata Umilitas and the 1342 San Miniato altarpieces. Thus, all three fall into the same dating span and they share many of the stylistic characteristics that define this period.

Millard Meiss, in his famous *Painting in Florence and Siena after the Black Death,* intent on differentiating between the artistic world of Giotto and that of the artists who belonged to the non-Giottesque world, lumped together the St. Cecilia Master, Pacino di Bonaguida, Jacopo del Casentino, and the Biadaiolo Master as "seeking an effect of greater animation and spontaneity, and a more fluid mode of expression";[16] and in a paragraph devoted to interpreting Frederick Antal, he noted the popular character of their art, aimed increasingly toward the middle and lower classes rather than the elite. With the exception of Pacino, Meiss's perceptions about those other artists seem just, although all of them flourished at a time much closer to the middle of the century than Meiss supposed.[17] It is with the same vocabulary of interpretation and applying the same spirit of the times that I believe we can best understand the St. Francis cycle at Assisi.

For the most part it would appear that the St. Francis cycle was painted at the end of the 1320s or the early part of the 1330s, based, in part, on borrowings from Giotto's frescoes in Santa Croce, Florence—not only those in the Bardi Chapel but also in the Peruzzi. On the other hand, it is generally agreed that a few of the scenes were executed at the very end of the campaign, including the first scene of *St. Francis Honored by a Simple Man,* as well as the last three, scenes XXVI–XXVIII, on the facing, or south, wall. The St. Cecilia Master is generally, although not universally, considered to be the author of these episodes that concluded the work on the cycle; Previtali has attributed the last four episodes to his "Montefalco Cross Master."[18]

Although the St. Cecilia Master may have taken up the project after the completion of the immediately preceding episodes, that is, after scene XXV, it is just as likely that there was another interruption before he started. That scene I, *St. Francis Honored by a Simple Man,* the first on the right, or north, wall, had apparently not yet been painted is certainly curious; the explanation must lie in Gnudi's proposal that the rood beam had not yet been installed.[19] The brackets for the beam, still embedded in the wall on either side of the fourth bay, were left there when the rood beam was demolished in 1623 to make room for a platform for an investiture ceremony.[20] As a result of the delay in installing the rood beam, the project may have been dormant for a period of unknown duration; after such an interval it would have been necessary to call in a new painter to finish the work, probably close to 1340.

Adjusting himself only a little to the style of his predecessors, the St. Cecilia Master created pictures in his own distinctive style, that is, close to that of his 1341 altarpiece for the Florentine church of Santa Cecilia. The choice of this specific artist for the work in Assisi would have been logical inasmuch as he may have been Roman by birth and possibly Roman in training. It was Offner who pointed out the consistent Roman undercurrent in his work, down to very specific details of style, and, especially, the influence of Cavallini's frescoes in the church of Santa Cecilia and of the Acquasparta Monument.[21] By and large, it appears that the decoration of the nave of the upper church was within the domain of the Roman school, with the exception of the Cimabuesque who painted the third and second bays on the south, or left, wall. In that case it would have been logical that a painter of Roman origin who happened to be working in Florence should have completed the cycle.

Very large stylistic differences between the St. Francis episodes from scenes II through XXV, on the one hand, and those that are attributed to the St. Cecilia Master go beyond the obviously elegant personal style of the master. For example, the *St. Francis Healing the Knight of Ilerda* (XXVI) has an ample, free architectural setting and a relatively small scale to the figures comparable to those in his St. Cecilia altarpiece. Furthermore, the new complexity of a room opening into other spaces both here and in the next scene, the *Confession of the Woman of Benevento,* scene XXVII (Fig. 27), suggests the artist's awareness of the grand, new spaciousness Giotto achieved in the *Ascension of St. John the Evangelist* (Fig. 40) and the *Annunciation to Zacharias* (Fig. 41) in the Peruzzi Chapel.

In the representation of architecture, the St. Cecilia Master did not merely take one step forward so much as leap ahead. For just about the first time he included actual, well-known buildings.[22] In the first scene of the cycle, St. Francis stands before a structure that has always been pleasurably recognized as the Roman Temple of Minerva, long since become the church of Santa Maria sopra Minerva, in the central piazza of Assisi (Fig. 73). During the course of the imitation the eight sturdy columns of the original structure became seven slender ones, yet the intent to bring the reality of Assisi into the picture cannot be doubted. The use of an actual building rendered with considerable verisimilitude is quite rare in art, probably for the very reason that the artist thereby abandoned the province of the imagination in favor of facsimilitude. Such illustration is, of course, the acme of the vernacular, and its usefulness in the St. Francis cycle cannot be overemphasized.

The Temple of Minerva is but one instance in which the St. Cecilia Master introduced the real world into these pictures. To the left of the temple in scene I is rendered the Palazzo del Capitano del Popolo, and between the two buildings is the Torre del Popolo; both are structures that still stand today. We have discussed elsewhere the old and worthless controversy over the supposed incompleteness of the tower in the fresco as a reason for dating the frescoes earlier than the time when the real tower was finished.[23] The artist recreated not just a building but the complex of structures at the center of Assisi, so that even the piazza itself where the action takes place is to be thought of as realized in the picture.

Across the nave in scene XXVIII, the episode of St. Francis liberating Peter of Alifia from prison, we have the same experience of being able to site the action of the drama, now in the city of Rome where the heretic, Peter, was arrested. We recognize a specific Roman monument: atop the prison on the right appears a representation of the Column of Trajan, with two spiral reliefs that depict on the one hand a raging battle and on the other what appears to be a harangue of the troops.

It would be difficult to identify the peculiar structure on the left of this same episode: the lower two levels consist of unadorned rectangles, while the third level consists of a row of niches containing statues (Fig. 99). The source for this must be the Florence Campanile (Fig. 100) that Giotto undertook in 1334 while he was Capomaestro of the cathedral.[24] Except for the bottom level, which Giotto executed before his death in 1337, the next three levels above are by his successor, Andrea Pisano. Of particular interest is the row of niches containing statues (Figs. 101 and 102).[25] To my knowledge, such an element had not previously been found in Italy and must have been directly inspired by the tower structures of such High Gothic churches as the cathedrals of Reims and Amiens where, several stories above ground, the Gallery of Kings sweeps outward from the central section of the facade onto the towers. By circa 1340, the Campanile niches would have been ready and perhaps the first of the statues installed.

The St. Cecilia Master would have known the state of the Campanile work at that point; further progress was to await the arrival on the scene of

99. (Above) St. Cecilia Master, *Prophets,* Detail of Scene XXVIII, Fig. 28, Upper Church, Assisi

100. (Left) Campanile of Florence Cathedral, Detail of Lower Section

101. (Above) Andrea Pisano, *Solomon,* Opera del Duomo, Florence
102. (Right) Andrea Pisano, *David,* Opera del Duomo, Florence

Talenti, around the middle of the century. In all probability, the St. Cecilia Master made a drawing of the structure in its partially completed state. Dependence on a drawing would explain the flattened-out quality of the design in the Assisi picture, in which the front and part of the left side are in the same plane. The projection represents the octagonal buttress at the corner of the Campanile, although the addition of niches in the Assisi fresco must be the artist's free interpretation of the original. Of course, the St. Cecilia Master had no idea how the elevation of the Campanile would be finished, and so he topped off his with the odd little tower. The style of the niche figures in the fresco at Assisi confirms the St. Cecilia Master's careful observation of Andrea Pisano's sculptures for the Campanile. Like the sculptor, the painter fills his niches with Old Testament figures, holding scrolls and turning and gesturing in a variety of ways.

All of these literal references to the real world that the St. Cecilia Master made—to the Temple of Minerva, the Torre del Popolo, the Palazzo del Capitano del Popolo, the Column of Trajan, and the partially built Florence Campanile—are at odds with the architecture in the rest of the St. Francis cycle. It suggests that the new artist called upon to finish these last four episodes may have come on the scene at some interval after the departure of the shop that had worked there earlier, so that he had no contact with them. Yet surely by about 1340 (before which I do not see how he could have started at Assisi) one might expect the newer, reality-oriented art of the contemporary scene. Like his predecessors, the St. Cecilia Master spoke in the vernacular language. But his version of popular art went farther than that of the originators of the St. Francis cycle, who would perhaps have found him excessive.

If then, as we suppose, the nave walls were finally covered with the fresco program and the campaign had at last come to a conclusion in the early 1340s, we are, to say the least, more and more curious about the 1345 date which was recently discovered inscribed in the passageway of the gallery between bay IV and bay III—the area above that of the last three scenes, XXVI, XXVII, and XXVIII—and which has been adjudged to be authentic.[26]

Once we agree that the St. Francis fresco series could have been completed as late as the early 1340s, we are encouraged to believe that its beginning could not have been so very far back in time as has usually been claimed. Therefore we incline to believe that whatever reasons brought about such a long delay after the painting of the choir and transepts by Cimabue, while the frescoes of the Old and New Testament series on the upper walls evolved, the St. Francis cycle appears to have been begun around 1330 and to have been completed only a decade later, in the early 1340s. In the course of this period, the nature of this "popular" art itself underwent a change, from an early approximation of the experiential world to a much more trustworthy, eyes-on-the-site, factual, even reportorial account of the actual world, in the last four scenes, which is furthermore presented as evidence for the reality of the events depicted in these episodes. Little wonder that the people of the fourteenth century found the cycle so appealing, directed as it was, not to some idealized, impossibly lofty, and almost incomprehensible world such as Giotto had depicted, but to a world that partook of the same life experiences as those of the spectators themselves.

NOTES

1. R. Offner, *A Critical and Historical Corpus of Florentine Painting*, sec. III, vol. II, part I, New York, 1930, 43–48, and plates XVIII[1] to XVIII.[9a]

2. Offner, ibid., sec. III, vol. II, part II, 88.

3. L. Dami, "La basilica di S. Miniato al Monte," *Bollettino d'arte*, 1915, IX, 217–44.

4. For details of the various scenes, see Offner, ibid., plates LIII–LIII.[9]

5. See L. Becherucci, *Encyclopedia of World Art*, IX, New York, 1959, 332, with a good review of the literature; and W. Cohn, "Contributo a Pietro Lorenzetti," *Rivista d'arte*, XXXIV, 1959, 3–17, with a strong defense of the early date.

6. DeWald also believed that the panel was not Sienese but Florentine, in which he was followed only by Giulia Sinibaldi—E. DeWald, "Pietro Lorenzetti," *Art Studies*, 1929, 131–66; G. Sinibaldi, *I Lorenzetti*, Siena, 1933, 109.

7. L. Marcucci, "La data della 'Santa Umiltà' di Pietro Lorenzetti," *Arte antica e moderna*, nos. 13–16, 1961, 21–26.

8. The primary authority for the St. Cecilia Master and one who did the most to integrate his oeuvre is Offner, *Corpus*, sec. III, vol. I, 1931. The lengthy discussion by A. Smart ("The St. Cecilia Master and His School at Assisi," *Burlington Magazine*, CII, 1960, 405–13, 430–37) is chiefly concerned with the notion that the St. Cecilia Master was the initiator of the cycle, an opinion that he later abandoned. The article by C. De Benedictus ("Nuove proposte per il Maestro della Santa Cecilia," *Antichità viva*, XI, no. 4, 1972, 3–9) is less helpful; the author added a poor frescoed *Madonna* to his oeuvre, placed the Montici *Madonna* at the end of the artist's career, and discarded Offner's theory of a Roman origin for the artist.

9. Offner, *Corpus*, sec. III, vol. I, 36–37, plates IX.[1–7]

10. Ibid., 26–28, plates VI–VI[2]; Florence: Commissione della mostra giottesca, *Pittura italiana del Duecento e Trecento, catalogo della mostra giottesca di Firenze del 1937*, eds. G. Sinibaldi and G. Brunetti, Florence, 1943, 392–93; A. Smart, *The Assisi Problem and the Art of Giotto*, Oxford, 1971, 33, 255.

11. Offner, *Corpus*, sec. III, vol. I, plates VIII.[1–4]

12. Ibid., sec. III, vol. II, part I, 32, plates VII–VII,[4] and sec. III, vol. VI, 1956, 3–7, 12; Smart, "St. Cecilia Master and His School," 431.

13. R. Oertel, "Giotto-Ausstellung," *Zeitschrift für Kunstgeschichte*, VI, 1937, 233–37 (and for the *Crucifix*, 224–33); G. Previtali, *Giotto e la sua bottega*, Milan, 1967, 58 and 136 n. 107.

14. Offner, *Corpus*, sec. III, vol. I, 24–26; Smart, *Assisi Problem*, 255, and "St. Cecilia Master and His School," 431.

15. P. Schubring, Review: G. Vithzum, *Bernardo Daddi*, in *Kunstchronik*, n.s., XV, 1904, col. 546; W. Suida, "Einige florentinische Maler aus der Zeit des Übergangs vom Dugento ins Trecento; der Cacilienalter der Uffizien," *Jahrbuch des preussischen Kunstsammlungen*, 1905, XXVI, 90.

16. M. Meiss, *Painting in Florence and Siena after the Black Death*, Princeton, 1951, 6.

17. Ibid., 173–74.

18. Previtali, *Giotto,* 51, 58, and 62.

19. C. Gnudi, *Giotto,* Milan, 1959, 66. See also L. Tintori and M. Meiss, *The Paintings of the Life of St. Francis in Assisi,* New York, 1962, 54; E. Baccheschi, *The Complete Paintings of Giotto,* New York, 1966, 91. Supino had the idea that the lost Giunta *Crucifix* of 1236 had been made for this rood beam, but the beam was evidently not installed until the early fourteenth century (*La basilica di S. Francesco di Assisi,* Bologna, 1924, 41).

20. L. Wadding, *Annales minorum seu trium ordinum a S. Francesco institutorum,* II, Rome, 1732, 397.

21. Offner, *Corpus,* sec. III, vol. I, xxi–iv, 15. See also Smart, "St. Cecilia Master and His School," 405–13, 430–37. His Roman origins are more fully explored by A. Parronchi, "Attività del 'Maestro di Santa Cecilia,' " *Rivista d'arte,* XXI, 1939, 193–228. For a refutation, see De Benedictus, "Nuove proposte," 3–9. Smart, in his discussion of the Tuscan origins of the St. Cecilia Master's art (*Assisi Problem,* 255–56), did not even refer to the Offnerian proposal of a Roman origin for the master.

22. See the illuminating article by John White: "Giotto's Use of Architecture in the 'Expulsion of Joachim' and 'The Entry into Jerusalem' at Padua," *Burlington Magazine,* CXV, 1973, 439–47. Such a fortress type as the Diocletian palace at Split could be used to suggest "Roman Jerusalem." This is not to say that it is representational in the sense in which we are speaking.

23. See the discussion in Chapter IV.

24. The comprehensive work on the subject of the Campanile is that of M. Trachtenberg, *The Campanile of Florence Cathedral. Giotto's Tower,* New York, 1971. Alastair Smart's idea that the structure on the left represented the Septizonium in Rome has the attraction that both buildings in scene XXVIII refer to Rome; thus, the story that began in Assisi ended in Rome (*Assisi Problem,* 23).

25. The statues by Andrea and his shop are illustrated in I. Toesca, *Andrea e Nino Pisano,* Florence, 1950, figs. 93–101, 103–106, and in *Il museo dell'Opera del Duomo a Firenze,* eds. L. Becherucci and G. Brunetti, 2 vols., Venice [1971?], plates 108–18.

26. J. White, "Cimabue and Assisi: Working Methods and Art Historical Consequences," *Art History,* IV, no. 4, 1981, 372–73. White said: "perhaps this place was forgotten and finished later at an unusually late stage in the work."

VIII

The Influence of the St. Francis Cycle

It would be surprising if so conspicuous and outstanding an example of the new vernacular style as the St. Francis cycle in the upper church at Assisi were not to have had a wide impact. And indeed, critics have been quick to point to examples of such an influence, particularly, of course, Giotto's Bardi Chapel frescoes of the 1320s. If we are correct in our assumption that the influence works the other way around, we would have to look for the impact of Assisi elsewhere and at a later date. Such instances are not difficult to find, as Dieter Blume has suggested in his recent book on Franciscan cycles.[1]

The choir of San Francesco in Pistoia is decorated with a series of twelve scenes from the Legend of St. Francis, a number of which borrow compositions and many details from Assisi, as has always been agreed.[2] Good examples of this are the episodes of the *Miracle of the Crucifix* (Fig. 103) and the *Dream of Innocent III* (Fig. 104), both lifted straight from the Assisi version. The artist, clearly a well-trained follower of Giotto, sometimes identified with Puccio Capanna, also had a good look at the frescoes in the Peruzzi Chapel—as in the architectural setting of the *Sermon to the Birds,* and in the setting of the *St. Francis Before the Sultan,* with the figure to the right slightly overlapped by the column as Giotto did it in the *Feast of Herod* (Fig. 42). The 1343 date that older writers saw in the now largely effaced inscription would suit the style of these frescoes very well.[3] This, in turn, is just when we might expect to see the influence of the Assisi Legend elsewhere. Contrariwise, it would be strange if no borrowings from so conspicuous a series of frescoes were to have been made for half a century.

Another series of Franciscan scenes imitating Assisi, which by its smooth sophistication appears to belong to the middle of the fourteenth century, is that of San Francesco, Rieti, north of Rome, the work of an Umbrian artist of considerable talent and one whose close adherence to certain compositional factors

103. Tuscan Painter, *Miracle of the Crucifix,* San Francesco, Pistoia

104. Tuscan Painter, *Dream of Innocent III,* San Francesco, Pistoia

in the Assisi cycle is startling.[4] Among a number of other cycles that adhere more or less closely to Assisi, all of which date to the middle of the fourteenth century or even later, are the following: San Francesco in San Genesio near Tolentino,[5] San Fortunato, Todi, in southern Umbria,[6] and Castelfiorentino between Florence and Siena.[7]

A Neapolitan panel whose whereabouts is unknown, and which is also attributed by Bologna to the Master of the Franciscan Tempere, is another

The altarpiece (Fig. 105) of the cathedral of Ottana, Sardinia, attributed by Ferdinando Bologna to the Master of the Franciscan Tempere (that is, linen paintings), was apparently made between 1338 and 1343 during the bishopric of Fra Silvestro.[8] Among the narratives on the panel is a *Stigmatization* that can only have derived from the one in the Assisi cycle: there are the two little huts and Leo sits in the lower right, book in his lap.[9] These characteristics first appear, as we have seen, in the upper church cycle. Other Assisi episodes are almost slavishly copied: the *Renunciation of Worldly Goods,* the *Dream of Innocent III,* and the *Vision of the Fiery Chariot.*[10]

A Neapolitan prayer book in the National Library, Vienna, that belonged to Joanna I of Naples also contains an illustration of the *Stigmatization* based on the Assisi scene.[11] Bologna dated the manuscript late (1362–75) because Joanna appears to be older than in her other illustrations; however, this may be a matter of the artist's style and, in fact, any date after her accession in 1343 is possible.

A Neapolitan panel whose whereabouts is unknown, and which is also attributed by Bologna to the Master of the Franciscan Tempere, is another

116

105. Master of the Franciscan Tempere, Altarpiece, Cathedral, Ottana, Sardinia

imitation of the *Stigmatization* fresco at Assisi.[12] Because St. Francis appears in a habit of patched materials such as the Spirituals affected—supposedly impossible after 1336, when Benedict XII ordered King Robert of Anjou to banish the Spirituals—Bologna wanted a date before 1336. This would suggest a borrowing from a very recent prototype.

We have seen from the cycle in the Pistoia cathedral that even a Giottesque painter could respond to the very different current represented by the vernacular art of the Legend at Assisi. And indeed, from the mid-1330s on, it must have been one of considerable fascination to Italian artists. Its influence is seen in another panel from Giotto's shop, the large *Stigmatization of St. Francis* (Fig. 106) in the Louvre.[13] In its predella three scenes derived from the Assisi Legend are represented: the *Dream of Innocent III* (Fig. 6); the *Sermon to the Birds* (Fig. 15); and the *Pope Honorius III Approving the Rule* [placed in the setting of the Assisi scene of *Pope Innocent III Sanctioning the Rule* (Fig. 7)]. Even though the panel bears the inscription "opus iocti florentini," not everyone attributes this fine panel to the master himself on account of its rather dry style, although we must suppose it came from Giotto's shop before his death in 1337.[14] It is revealing to compare it to the somewhat earlier *Stigmatization of St. Francis* (Fig. 107) in the

106. Giotto Shop, *Stigmatization of St. Francis,* Louvre, Paris

107. Taddeo Gaddi in Giotto's Shop, *Stigmatization of St. Francis,* Fogg Museum, Cambridge, Mass.

Fogg Museum, Cambridge, which is nowadays seen to be one of Taddeo Gaddi's first works, but which was done, I should say, in Giotto's shop so close is it to the spirit of the Bardi Chapel *Stigmatization* (Fig. 39).[15] Although none of the various representations of the theme repeats Giotto's enormously complex posture of the saint's figure, the Fogg panel follows the Bardi Chapel version in a number of ways: the cave on the hill, the position of the Seraphic Christ turned toward the saint, and the presence of but a single chapel, the one in the lower right corner.

Looking again at the later Louvre panel, we see that the artist has imitated Assisi with its two huts, and in the more frontal Seraphic Christ, as well as, of course, the three imitations of Assisi narratives in the predella. Unlike the Neapolitan versions of the Assisi *Stigmatization of St. Francis* (Fig. 19), none of the Giottesque ones includes the figure of Brother Leo. Following the presumed success of the Bardi Chapel decoration, it would appear that the Giotto shop was called upon for interpretations of the *Stigmatization.* By the mid-1330s, when the master was preoccupied with larger schemes, we suppose an assistant could have been inspired by the new series at Assisi, and, deviating from the standard Giotto composition, created what we see in the Louvre panel.

The Taddeo Gaddi *armadio* of the Santa Croce sacristy, already mentioned, on which he painted scenes from the Life of Christ and the Legend of St. Francis, probably around 1335, is of especial interest to us here.[16] Taddeo kept close to the formulas of his old master, Giotto, wherever he was able to, glancing now and again at the grand prototypes in the Bardi Chapel. Thus the *Apparition at Arles* (Fig. 108) and the *Death and Ascension of St. Francis* follow the Bardi compositions. On the other hand, there are a number of episodes where the solution was taken from Assisi: the *Dream of Innocent III* (Fig. 109) and the *Vision of the Fiery Chariot* (Fig. 110) tell us in no uncertain terms that Taddeo was highly susceptible to the inventive, veristic style of Assisi. Then, too, although the *Christmas Crib at Greccio* (Fig. 111) can hardly be said to copy the one at Assisi, the intriguing view behind the altar suggests Taddeo's awareness of that sort of vernacular expression so often to be found in Assisi.[17]

In the examples we have adduced here, it appears as though the Assisi St. Francis cycle had its first major impact between around 1335 and 1345. Fresco cycles in Pistoia, Rieti, Todi, and other Franciscan churches, two Neapolitan panel paintings and a Neapolitan manuscript, a panel from Giotto's shop, as well as a St. Francis cycle by Giotto's foremost pupil, Taddeo Gaddi, are all to be dated within this time frame, and all represent variants on Assisi. Thus, around the middle of the fourteenth century and into the third quarter, a good number of cycles were created that always acknowledged the priority and authority of the

108. Taddeo Gaddi, *Apparition at Arles,* Galleria dell'Accademia, Florence

109. Taddeo Gaddi, *Dream of Innocent III,* Galleria dell'Accademia, Florence

110. Taddeo Gaddi, *Vision of the Fiery Chariot,* Galleria dell'Accademia, Florence

111. Taddeo Gaddi, *Christmas Crib at Greccio,* Galleria dell'Accademia, Florence

Legend at Assisi. Surely this is to be taken as evidence of the late date of the St. Francis paintings in Assisi. Were these Assisi prototypes to have been painted at the end of the Dugento, as many would have us believe, we would be surprised to discover that their impact and the wide diffusion of their imagery were only registered so many years later. Blume has been the first to study thoroughly mural paintings of the St. Francis Legend as a propaganda device of the Franciscan Order, but his adherence to an early date in the 1290s for the Assisi Legend prevents the clear focus on this development that is arrived at only when the Assisi Legend is seen as a much later work.

In recent years, the problem of the St. Nicholas Chapel in the lower church has been confounded by the widespread belief that its decoration had to have been earlier than 1307 on account of the similarity between the *St. Clare* (Fig. 114) on the entry arch of the chapel and the one in the altarpiece (Fig. 76) in the Gardner Museum, Boston, signed and dated by Giuliano da Rimini.[18] We have elsewhere discussed the unlikelihood that this date on the panel painting is original. Still, it has become popular to date almost everything in the upper and lower churches at Assisi on the basis of that St. Clare, and also, as John White had already theorized, on the St. Francis figure in the Gardner panel's *Stigmatization of St. Francis* (Fig. 77), which so resembles the one in the *Stigmatization* (Fig. 19) in the upper church cycle.[19]

Because of the weight that has been given to the dating of the St. Nicholas Chapel in recent literature, it seems appropriate to explore here the problems and misunderstandings about the chapel in a little detail. Igino Supino clearly demonstrated that the chapel was dedicated jointly to Gian Gaetano Orsini, more commonly called Giovanni, who died between 1292 and 1294, and was buried in the chapel, and to his brother, Cardinal Napoleone Orsini, who died many years later, in 1342, after he had had the St. Nicholas Chapel decorated as a monument to his long-dead brother Giovanni.[20] And it is these brothers who are represented in the stained-glass window of the chapel.[21]

Although the *Apostles* (Figs. 112 and 113) that decorate the lower part of the wall in the St. Nicholas Chapel are clearly Giottesque, and indeed in the Paduan manner, as Previtali rightly pointed out,[22] we may presume that that part of the decoration was accomplished at an earlier date than the St. Nicholas cycle. One can believe that the *Apostles* were painted soon after Giotto and his shop had completed their frescoes (Figs. 71 and 72) in the Magdalen Chapel which, as we said earlier, must have been by early 1309. No doubt Cardinal Napoleone began the decoration of his brother's tomb chapel by the end of the first decade and did not pick up on the program of decoration until much later, when the

112. *Apostle,* St. Nicholas Chapel, Lower Church, Assisi

113. *Apostle,* St. Nicholas Chapel, Lower Church, Assisi

St. Nicholas cycle was executed—probably not before the middle of the 1330s, as the cardinal aged and his own mortality came more and more into his consciousness. Robin Simon has introduced structural evidence to prove that the St. Nicholas Chapel was built after the Magdalen Chapel.[23] Consequently, a different sequence of events becomes clear to us. First, the Magdalen Chapel was built and decorated; then the St. Nicholas Chapel was built and decorated only in part. Its completion was not accomplished until the 1330s: at that time the Nicholas cycle and the saints including *St. Clare* (Figs. 114 and 115) on the inner face of the entrance arch were painted.

It is possible that the tomb of Gian Gaetano (Fig. 116) was created at this

114. *St. Clare*, St. Nicholas Chapel, Lower Church, Assisi

115. *St. Sabinus*, St. Nicholas Chapel, Lower Church, Assisi

later time, in which case the body would have been transferred from whatever tomb it had occupied. Opinions on the authorship vary widely. For Adolfo Venturi, the tomb was by Giovanni da Cosma of Rome early in the century; Beda Kleinschmidt gave it to a follower of his, although the absence of the ubiquitous cosmatesque decoration should have discouraged such an idea.[24] Supino followed

116. Tomb of Gian Gaetano Orsini, St. Nicholas Chapel, Lower Church, Assisi

Filippini's suggestion that the sculptor was one who worked for the Orsini in the 1330s, the Roman Giovanni Salvati of whom no other works survive.[25] Vasari attributed it to Agnolo di Ventura of Siena, who flourished in the 1330s and 1340s.[26] Another proposal involved pupils of Lorenzo Maitani.[27] But in any case, nothing conclusive demands that we date the tomb in the 1290s or in the first twenty years of the Trecento. Just the fluidity of form comparable to what one finds in, for example, Tino da Camaino of the 1320s should suggest caution about dating the Orsini monument too early in the century.[28] If it were in fact done later, the chapel may have undergone a belated and elaborate embellishment in the latter half of the 1330s, as the St. Nicholas paintings themselves suggest.

The lateness of the paintings in the St. Nicholas Legend can be easily ascertained. In the scene of the *St. Nicholas Thanked by the Knights He Saved* (Fig. 117), the setting is a church facade that is nothing more than a reprise of the church from which the Poor Clares rushed to attend the bier of St. Francis in the upper church (XXIII); the artist was moved by an identical urge to heap decorative detail on the facade as a means of persuading us of its reality. In the

124

117. *St. Nicholas Thanked by the Knights He Saved,* St. Nicholas Chapel, Lower Church, Assisi

118. *St. Nicholas Appearing to Constantine in a Dream,* St. Nicholas Chapel, Lower Church, Assisi

St. Nicholas Appearing to Constantine in a Dream (Fig. 118), one is riveted by the details of the emperor's chamber and the dungeon below, with its prisoners peering out. How could it be imagined that the spatial complexities and veristic interests of the *St. Nicholas Appearing to Constantine in a Dream* could emerge before 1307? Clearly, such contrivings ought to be placed at a time after Giotto's Peruzzi Chapel as well as the upper church Legend. The *St. Nicholas Returns the Youth Adeodato to His Family* (Fig. 119), with its plethora of table objects, the grain and knots of the platform, as well as the note of bustling domesticity, comes close to Taddeo Gaddi's *St. Louis of Toulouse Serving the Poor* (Fig. 85), one of the scenes surrounding his *Tree of Life* fresco of the 1330s in the Santa Croce refectory. But more than these details draws these two narratives together in the same decade: it is the psychic interchanges reverberating back and forth among the figures. And that, it seems to me, is one of the great qualities Giotto introduced into the frescoes of the Peruzzi Chapel.

These narratives were made by artists who were entranced by the new verism of the St. Francis Legend in the upper church, even exaggerating its

125

119. *St. Nicholas Returns the Youth Adeodato to His Family,* St. Nicholas Chapel, Lower Church, Assisi

120. Riminese Painter, *Miraculous Supper of St. Guido,* Refectory, Abbey of Pomposa

colloquial dialogue. Still, it would be parochial to make too precise connections here. The artistic modes we have been describing were widespread by the second half of the 1330s, as we see so vividly in the narratives of Taddeo Gaddi's Baroncelli frescoes (Fig. 83), his *armadio* series (Figs. 108–111), and his *Tree of Life* (Figs. 84 and 85), all datable to that decade. Nor should we overlook the *Good Government* frescoes (Fig. 90) by Ambrogio Lorenzetti from the end of the 1330s. Furthermore, it is only a short reach to such lively scenes as those in the refectory of Pomposa (Fig. 120), or the St. Nicholas Chapel at Tolentino (Fig. 80), both important monuments of Riminese art of the 1340s.[29] While one or a number of Riminese artists were familiar with the St. Francis cycle at Assisi, it is just as likely that they simply shared the new vernacular imagery that began in the 1330s and was everywhere by the 1340s.

NOTES

1. D. Blume, *Wandmalerei als Ordenspropaganda, Bildprogramme im Chorbereich franziskanischer Konvente Italiens bis zur Mitte des 14. Jahrhunderts,* Worms, 1983.

2. A. Chiappelli, "Puccio Capanna e gli affreschi in San Francesco a Pistoia," *Dedalo,* X, 199–228; O. Sirén, *Giotto and Some of His Followers,* I, Cambridge (Mass.), 1917, 125–29. For a modern résumé, see Blume, *Wandmalerei als Ordenspropaganda,* 49–54, 161–62, figs. 107–11, and A. Smart, *The Assisi Problem and the Art of Giotto,* Oxford, 1971, 109.

3. S. Ciampi, *Notizie inedite della sagrestia pistoiese de' belli arredi del camposanto pisano e di altre opere di disegno dal secolo XII al XV,* Florence, 1810, 103.

4. Blume, *Wandmalerei als Ordenspropaganda,* 42–45, 163–71, figs. 90, 91, and 94. Blume adhered to an early date for this cycle, circa 1295.

5. Ibid., 63–64, figs. 151, 154, and 155.

6. Ibid., 54–57, fig. 133.

7. Ibid., 65–66, fig. 157.

8. F. Bologna, *I pittori alle corte angioina di Napoli, 1266–1414, e un riesamo dell'arte nell'età fridericiana,* Rome, 1969, figs. VI-18 to VI-37, colorplates XI–XXIII.

9. Bologna gave no detail of this scene, but it is visible in the photograph of the entire panel, fig. VI-18.

10. These narratives occupy the left-hand side of the altarpiece; the narrative sequence on the right is of St. Nicholas. Among these episodes is the *Restoration of the Child to His Parents,* which quite thoroughly copies the same episode in the St. Nicholas Chapel in the lower church of the 1330s (Bologna, *Corte angioina,* fig. VI-27 and colorplate XXIII).

11. Bologna, ibid., captions with figs. VI-68, VI-69; illustrated in H. J. Hermann, *Die italienischen Handschriften des Dugento und Trecento,* in *Be-*

schreibendes Verzeichnis der illuminierten Handschriften in Oesterreich, Leipzig, 1930, sec. VIII, vol. V, part 3, fig. C (2), and see text 231, 243.

12. Bologna, *Corte angioina,* colorplate XVIII and fig. VI-3 with caption.

13. J. Gardner, "The Louvre Stigmatization and the Problem of the Narrative Altarpiece," *Zeitschrift für Kunstgeschichte,* XLV, 1982, 217–47; Smart, *Assisi Problem,* 109–11.

14. For the most recent discussion of the attribution, see Gardner, "The Louvre Stigmatization," 231 and n. 56.

15. A. Ladis, *Taddeo Gaddi, Critical Reappraisals and Catalogue Raisonné,* Columbia, Mo., and London, 1982, 18–19, cat. 3; see also Previtali, *Giotto e la sua bottega,* Milan, 1967, 45, caption for fig. 61.

16. Florence: Commissione della mostra giottesca, *Pittura italiana del Duecento e Trecento, catalogo della mostra giottesca di Firenze del 1937,* eds. G. Sinibaldi and G. Brunetti, Florence, 1943, 429–42; for all the St. Francis episodes, see figs. 137^P–137^y.

17. Inasmuch as Taddeo could include more narratives than Giotto in his limited program, he looked to Assisi also in selecting both the *Pope Innocent III Sanctioning the Rule* and the *Honorius III Approving the Rule.* Giotto had depicted only the latter subject.

18. When Meiss advanced the notion that the St. Clare in Giuliano's altarpiece with the 1307 date was based on the one in the St. Nicholas Chapel, he was forced to abandon his previously held belief that the frescoes in the chapel dated to circa 1310–15 *(Giotto and Assisi, New York, 1960, 3–4).* Meiss also thought the Crucifix in the *Miracle of the Crucifix,* scene IV, was the inspiration for the 1308 dated altarpiece by the so-called Cesi Master ("Reflections of Assisi: A Tabernacle and the Cesi Master," in *Scritti di storia dell'arte in onore di Mario Salmi,* II, Rome, 1962, 75–111, esp. 104–106). Although Smart thought the fresco had a common Romanesque prototype, as in the example by Sozio in Spoleto, he agreed with Meiss that the Cesi Master got his inspiration from the fresco. Of course, it would have been just as likely that the Cesi Master looked at an original cross *(Assisi Problem,* 162).

19. J. White, "The Date of 'The Legend of St. Francis' at Assisi," *Burlington Magazine,* XVIIIC, 1956, 344–51. Meiss supposed a reliance on two other of the saints on the entry arch by the author

of the altarpiece dated 1308 in the Cesi Duomo (Meiss, *Giotto and Assisi,* 4).

20. I. B. Supino, "La cappella di Gian Gaetano Orsini nella basilica di San Francesco d'Assisi," *Bollettino d'arte,* VI, 1926–27, 131–35. In effect, Supino disproved the older theory that the chapel had been dedicated to a cousin of the brothers, also named Gian Gaetano Orsini, who died in 1335 and was interred in St. Peter's, Rome. See also H. Maginnis, "Assisi Revisited: Notes on Recent Observations," *Burlington Magazine,* CXVII, 1975, 511–17.

21. G. Marchini, *L'Umbria,* vol. I in *Corpus vitrearum medii aevi, Italia,* Rome, 1973, 98–106, plates LXXV (entire central window), LXXVI (Napoleone Orsini and St. Nicholas), and LXXIX (Gian Gaetano Orsini presented by St. Francis).

22. G. Previtali, *Giotto e la sua bottega,* Milan, 1967, 85.

23. R. Simon, "Towards a Relative Chronology of the Frescoes in the Lower Church of San Francesco in Assisi," *Burlington Magazine,* CXVIII, 1976, 361–66.

24. A. Venturi, *Storia dell'arte italiana,* IV, Milan, 1906, 142; B. Kleinschmidt, *Die Basilika San Francesco in Assisi,* II, Berlin, 1926, 153. J. Gardner saw the Orsini tomb as a continuation of the prototypical tomb of Boniface VIII by Arnolfo di Cambio, as indeed it is, although executed at a much later time. His belief in the 1307 date for the St. Nicholas Chapel decoration may have influenced his opinions —"Arnolfo di Cambio and Roman Tomb Design," *Burlington Magazine,* CXV, 1973, 420–39.

25. I. B. Supino, *Giotto,* I, Florence, 1920, 196–98; L. Filippini, *La scultura nel Trecento in Roma,* Turin, 1908, 84, 86, and 91.

26. G. Vasari, *Le vite de più eccellenti pittori, scultori ed architettori,* ed. Milanesi, I, Florence, 1878, 439. The reference occurs in his lengthy joint "life" of Agnolo and another Sienese artist, Agostino di Giovanni, which runs from pp. 429 to 445.

27. Touring Club Italiano, *Umbria,* Milan, 1978, 126.

28. One thinks of the tomb of Carlo, duke of Calabria, in Santa Chiara, Naples (ca. 1325), and that of Queen Mary of Hungary in Santa Maria Donnaregina (E. Lavagnino, *Storia dell'arte medioevale italiana,* Turin, 1936, figs. 552 and 551).

29. The refectory at Pomposa was not built until

1320, so the frescoes are necessarily later; they have been attributed variously to Baronzio, Pietro da Rimini, and others (M. Bonicatti, *Trecentisti riminese: sulla formazione della pittura riminese del' 300,* Rome, 1963, 41, 82). C. Volpe gave a careful scrutiny to the St. Nicholas Chapel in the cathedral of Tolentino and dated the frescoes there between 1335–48; the chapel was dedicated in the latter year (*La pittura riminese del Trecento,* Milan, 1965, 45–48). F. Zeri, in pointing out different hands at work in Tolentino, especially that of Pietro, said it was too soon to decide whether Longhi had been correct in saying (in a lecture at Bologna) that some of it represented a late phase of Giuliano ("Una 'Deposizione' di scuola riminese," *Paragone,* no. 99, 1958, 50); see Chapter IV, note 29.

Bibliography

Aubert, A. *Die malerische Dekoration der San Francesco Kirche in Assisi: Ein Beitrag zur Lösung der Cimabue Frage,* Leipzig, 1907.

Baccheschi, E., *The Complete Paintings of Giotto,* New York, 1966.

Battisti, E., *Giotto, Biographical and Critical Study,* Lausanne, 1960.

Becherucci, L., in *Encyclopedia of World Art,* IX, New York, 1959, 332.

Bellosi, L., "La barba di S. Francesco (nuove proposte per il problema di Assisi)," *Prospettiva,* 1980, no. 22, 11–34.

Belting, H., *Die Oberkirche von San Francesco in Assisi: ihre Dekoration als Aufgabe und die Genese einer neuen Wandmalerei,* Berlin, 1977.

Bertelli, C., "La Mostra degli affreschi di Grottaferrata," *Paragone,* no. 249, 1970, 91–101.

Beyle, M. H. (Stendhal), *Histoire de la peinture en Italie,* in *Oeuvres complètes de Stendhal,* III, Paris, 1953.

Blume, D., *Wandmalerei als Ordenspropaganda: Bildprogramme im Chorbereich franziskanischer Konvente Italiens bis zur Mitte des 14. Jahrhunderts,* Worms, 1983.

Bonicatti, M., *Trecentisti riminese: sulla formazione della pittura riminese del '300,* Rome, 1963.

Bologna, F., "Ciò che resta di un capolavoro giovanile di Duccio," *Paragone,* no. 125, 1960, 3–31.

———, *Early Italian Painting, Romanesque and Early Medieval Art,* Princeton, 1964.

———, *I pittori alla corte angioina di Napoli, 1266–1414, e un riesamo dell'arte nell'età fridericiana,* Rome, 1969.

———, *Novità su Giotto, Giotto al tempo della cappella Peruzzi,* Turin, 1969.

Bonaventure, St., *Legendae Duae,* Quaracchi, 1898, 1923.

Borsook, E., *The Mural Painters of Tuscany from Cimabue to Andrea del Sarto,* London, 1960; 2nd rev. ed., Oxford and New York, 1980.

———, "Notizie su due cappelle in Santa Croce a Firenze," *Rivista d'arte,* XXXVI, 1961–62, 89–107.

Boskovits, M., "Celebrazioni dell' VIII centenario della nascità di San Francesco, studi recenti sulla basilica di Assisi," *Arte cristiani,* n.s., LXXI, 1983, no. 697, 203–14.

———, *Pittura fiorentina alla vigilia del Rinascimento,* Florence, 1975.

———, "Nuovi studi su Giotto e Assisi," *Paragone,* no. 261, 1971, 34–56.

Bracaloni, P. Leone, "Assisi medioevale: studio storico-topografico," *Archivum franciscanum historicum,* VII, 1909, 3–19.

Brandi, C., *Giotto,* Milan, 1983.

———, "Sulla chronologia degli affreschi della chiesa superiore in Assisi," *Giotto e il suo tempo,* in *Atti del congresso internazionale per la celebrazione del VII centenario della nascità di Giotto, 24 settembre–1 ottobre 1967, Assisi-Padova-Firenze,* Rome, 1971, 61–66.

Brunetti, G., "Note sul soggiorno fiorentino di Tino," *Commentari,* III, 1952, 97–107.

Bughetti, B., "Una parziale nuova traduzione degli Actus accopiata ad alcuni capitoli dei Fioretti," *Archivum franciscanum historicum,* XXI, 1928, 515–52, and XXII, 1929, 63–113.

Cecchelli, C., *I mosaici della basilica di S. Maria Maggiore,* Turin, 1956.

Cecchi, E., *Giotto,* Milan, 1937; 2nd ed., Milan, 1942; English trans., New York, Toronto, and London, 1960.

Censi, C., *Documentazione di vita assisiana, 1300–1448,* Grottaferrata, 1974.

Chiappelli, A., "Puccio Capanna e gli affreschi in San Francesco a Pistoia," *Dedalo,* X, 1929, 199–228.

Ciampi, S., *Notizie inedite della sagrestia pistoiese de' belli arredi del camposanto pisano e di altre opere di disegno dal secolo XII al XV,* Florence, 1810.

Cohn, W., "Contributo a Pietro Lorenzetti," *Rivista d'arte,* XXXIV, 1959, 3–17.

Coletti, L., *Gli affreschi della basilica di Assisi,* Bergamo, 1949.

Dami, L., "La basilica di S. Miniato al Monte," *Bollettino d'arte,* IX, 1915, 217–44.

De Benedictus, C., "Nuove proposte per il Maestro della Santa Cecilia," *Antichità viva,* XI, no. 4, 1972, 3–9.

DeWald, E., "Pietro Lorenzetti," *Art Studies,* VII, 1929, 131–66.

Donati, P. P., *Taddeo Gaddi,* Florence, 1966.

Dvořak, M., *Idealism and Naturalism in Gothic Art,* Notre Dame, Ind., 1967 (translated from *Idealismus und Naturalismus in der gotischen Sculptur und Malerei,* Munich, 1918).

Fleming, J. V., *From Bonaventure to Bellini, an Essay in Franciscan Exegesis,* Princeton, 1982.

Florence: Commissione della mostra giottesca, *Pittura italiana del Duecento e Trecento, catalogo della mostra giottesca del 1937,* eds. G. Sinibaldi and G. Brunetti, Florence, 1943.

Florence: Opera del Duomo, *Il museo dell'Opera del Duomo a Firenze,* eds. L. Becherucci and G. Brunetti, 2 vols., Venice [1971].

Fava, D., *Emilia e Romagna,* Milan, 1932.

Fisher, M. R., "Assisi, Padua, and the Boy in the Tree," *Art Bulletin,* XXXVIII, 1956, 47–52.

Fratini, G., *Storia della Basilica e del Convento di S. Francesco in Assisi,* Prato, 1882.

Gabrielli, M., *Giotto e l'origine del realismo,* Rome, 1960; 2nd revised ed., Rome, 1981.

———, *Il ciclo francescano di Assisi: considerazioni stilistiche e storico-teologiche,* Florence, 1970.

Gamba, C., "Osservazioni sull'arte di Giotto," *Rivista d'arte,* XIX, 1937, 271–85.

Gardner, J., "Arnolfo di Cambio and Roman Tomb Design," *Burlington Magazine,* CXV, 1973, 420–39.

———, "The Decoration of the Baroncelli Chapel in Santa Croce," *Zeitschrift für Kunstgeschichte,* XXXIV, 1971, 89–113.

———, "The Louvre Stigmatization and the Problem of the Narrative Altarpiece," *Zeitschrift für Kunstgeschichte,* XLV, 1982, 217–47.

———, "Pope Nicholas IV and the Decoration of Santa Maria Maggiore," *Zeitschrift für Kunstgeschichte,* XXXVI, 1973, 1–50.

———, "S. Paolo fuori le mura, Nicholas III, and Pietro Cavallini," *Zeitschrift für Kunstgeschichte,"* XXXIV, 1971, 240–48.

Ghiberti, L., *I commentari,* ed. O. Morisani, Naples, 1947.

Giglio-Tos, E., *La basilica d'Assisi,* Assisi, 1928.

Gnudi, C., "Il passo di Riccobaldo Ferrarese relativo a Giotto e il problema della sua autenticità," in *Studies in the History of Art Dedicated to William E. Suida on His Eightieth Birthday,* London, 1959, 26–30.

———, *Giotto,* Milan, 1959.

Goetz, W., *Assisi,* Leipzig, 1909.

Gosebruch, M., "Gli affreschi di Giotto nel braccio destro del transetto e nelle 'vele' centrali della chiesa inferiore di San Francesco," in *Giotto e i giotteschi in Assisi,* ed. G. Palumbo, Rome, 1969, 129–98.

———, *Giotto und die Entwicklung des neuzeitlichen Kunstbewusstseins,* Cologne, 1962.

———, "Sulla necessità di colmare la lacuna tra Padova e le cappelle di S. Croce nella biografia artistica di Giotto," *Giotto e il suo tempo,* in *Atti del congresso internazionale per la celebrazione del VII centenario della nascità di Giotto, 24 settembre–1 ottobre, 1967, Assisi-Padova-Firenze,* Rome, 1971, 233–51.

Gotti, A., *Del trionfo di San Tommaso d'Aquino, dipinto nel cappellone degli Spagnoli, antico capitolo de' frati di Santa Maria Novella in Firenze,* Florence, 1887.

Habig, M., *St. Francis of Assisi: Writings and Early Biographies; English Omnibus of the Sources for the Life of St. Francis,* 3rd revised ed., Chicago, 1973.

Hausenstein, W., *Giotto,* Berlin, 1923.

Hauser, A., *The Social History of Art,* 2 vols., New York, 1951.

Hendy, P., *European and American Paintings in the Isabella Stewart Gardner Museum,* Boston, 1974.

Henkels, H., "Remarks on the Late XIII Century Apse Decoration in Santa Maria Maggiore," *Simiolus,* IV, no. 3, 1971, 128–49.

Hermanin, F., "Le pitture dei monasteri sublacensi," in *I monasteri di Subiaco,* ed. P. Egidi, 2 vols., Rome, 1904.

Hermann, H. J., *Die italienischen Handscriften des Dugento und Trecento* in *Beschreibendes Verzeichnis der illuminierten Handschriften in Oesterreich,* Leipzig, 1930, sec. VIII, vol. V.

Hertlein, A., *Die Basilika San Francesco in Assisi: Gestalt, Bedeutung, Herkunft,* Florence, 1964.

Hetherington, P., *Pietro Cavallini: A Study in the Art of Late Medieval Rome,* London, 1979.

————, "Pietro Cavallini, Artistic Style and Patronage in Late Medieval Rome," *Burlington Magazine,* CXIV, 1972, 4–10.

Hueck, I., "Der Maler des Apostelszenen im Atrium von Alt-St.Peter," *Mitteilungen des kunsthistorischen Institutes in Florenz,* XIV, 1969, 115–44.

Isermeyer, C. A., *Rahmengliederung und Bildfolge in der Wandmalerei bei Giotto und den florentiner Malern des 14. Jahrhunderts,* Würzburg, 1937.

Kleinschmidt, B., *Das Basilika San Francesco in Assisi,* 3 vols., Berlin, 1915–28.

Klesse, B., *Seidenstoffe in der italienischen Malerei des 14. Jahrhunderts,* Bern, 1967.

Kruft, H.-W., Review: Previtali, *Giotto e la sua bottega,* in *Zeitschrift für Kunstgeschichte,* XXXII, 1969, 47–51.

Laderchi, C., "Giotto," *Nuova Antologia,* VI, 1867, 31–62.

Ladis, A., *Taddeo Gaddi, Critical Reappraisals and Catalogue Raisonné,* Columbia, Mo., and London, 1982.

Lanzi, L., *Storia pittorica dell'Italia dal risorgimento delle belle arti fin presso la fina del XVIII secolo,* 6 vols., Bolzano, 1789.

Little, A., "Description of a Franciscan Manuscript Formerly in the Phillips Library," *British Society of Franciscan Studies, Collectanae Franciscana,* V, 1914, 9–113.

Lochoff, L., "Gli affreschi dell'antico e nuovo testamento nella basilica superiore di Assisi," *Rivista d'arte,* XVI, 1937, 240–70.

Longhi, R., "Giudizio sul duecento," *Proporzioni,* II, 1948, 5–54.

Maginnis, H., "Assisi Revisited: Notes on Recent Observations," *Burlington Magazine,* CXVII, 1975, 511–17.

————, "The Passion Cycle in the Lower Church of San Francesco, Assisi: The Technical Evidence," *Zeitschrift für Kunstgeschichte,* XXXIX, 1976, 193–208.

Mallory, M., "Thoughts Concerning the 'Master of the Glorification of St. Thomas,'" *Art Bulletin,* LVII, 1975, 9–20.

Marchini, G., "Le vetrate della Basilica di San Francesco," in *Giotto e i giotteschi in Assisi,* ed. G. Palumbo, Rome, 1969, 271–99.

————, *L'Umbria* in *Corpus vitrearum medii aevi, Italia,* vol. I, Rome, 1973.

Marcucci, L., "La data della 'Santa Umilita' di Pietro Lorenzetti," *Arte antica e moderna,* nos. 13–16, 1961, 21–26.

————, "Per gli 'armarj' della sacrestia di Santa Croce," *Mitteilungen des kunsthistorischen Institutes in Florenz,* IX, 1960, 141–58.

Mariani, V., "Giotto nel ciclo della 'Vita di San Francesco,'" in *Giotto e i giotteschi,* ed. G. Palumbo, Rome, 1969, 61–92.

Marinangeli, B., "Giotto nella basilica di Assisi," *Miscellanea francescana,* XXXVII, 1937, 5–59.

————, "Le serie d'affreschi giotteschi rappresentante la vita di S. Francesco," *Miscellanea francescana,* XIII, 1911, 97ff.

Marle, R. van, *The Development of the Italian Schools of Painting,* 19 vols., The Hague, 1923–38.

————, *La peinture romaine au moyen-âge, son développement du 6ème jusqu'à la fin du 13ème siècle,* Strasbourg, 1921.

Martinelli, V., "Un documento per Giotto ad Assisi," *Storia dell'arte,* XIX, 1973, 193–208.

Martius, L., *Die Franziskuslegende in der Oberkirche von S. Francesco zu Assisi,* Berlin, 1932.

Matthiae, G., *Pittura romana del medioevo,* 2 vols., Rome, 1965–66.

————, *Pietro Cavallini,* Rome, 1972.

————, "Le arte plastiche e figurative," in *Arte, scienze e cultura in Roma cristiana,* by Mariano da Alatri, Isidoro da Villapadierna, and others, Bologna, 1971, 15–99.

————, *S. Lorenzo fuori le mura,* Rome, 1966 [Le chiese di Roma illustrate, no. 89].

Meiss, M., *Giotto and Assisi,* New York, 1960.

————, *Painting in Florence and Siena after the Black Death,* Princeton, 1951.

————, "Reflections of Assisi: A Tabernacle and the Cesi Master," *Scritti di storia dell'arte in onore di Mario Salmi,* Rome, 1962, II, 75–111.

Mitchell, C., "The Imagery of the Upper Church at Assisi," *Giotto e il suo tempo,* in *Atti del congresso internazionale per la celebrazione del VII centenario della nascità di Giotto, 24 settembre–1 ottobre 1967, Assisi-Padova-Firenze,* Rome, 1971, 113–34.

————, "The Lateran Fresco of Boniface VIII," *Journal of the Warburg and Courtauld Institutes,* XIV, 1951, 1–6.

Moltesen, E., *Giotto und die Meister der Franzlegende,* Copenhagen, 1930.

Mommsen, T., *Petrarch's Testament,* Ithaca, N.Y., 1957.

Moorman, J. R. H., "Early Franciscan Art and Literature," *Bulletin of the John Rylands Library, Manchester,* XXVII, 1942–43, 338–58.

Moschetti, A., *Bollettino del Museo Civico di Padova,* 1931, 201.

Munoz, A., *La basilica di S. Lorenzo fuori le mura,* Rome [1944].

Muratori, L. A., *Rerum italicarum scriptores; raccolta degli storici italiani dal cinquecento al millecinquecento,* IX, Città di Castello, 1900.

Murray, P., "Ghiberti e il suo secondo Commentario," in *Lorenzo Ghiberti nel suo tempo. Atti del convegno internazionale di studi; Firenze, 18–21 ottobre, 1978,* Florence, 1980, II, 283–92.

————, "Notes on Some Early Giotto Sources," *Journal of the Warburg and Courtauld Institutes,* XVI, 1953, 58–80.

Newton, F., *St. Francis and His Basilica,* Assisi, 1926.

Oakeshott, W., *The Mosaics of Rome,* Greenwich, Conn., 1967.

Oertel, R., *Early Italian Painting to 1400,* London [ca. 1968] (original German edition, 1953).

————, "Giotto-Ausstellung in Florenz: II. Zu Giottos vorpaduanischem Stil," *Zeitschrift für Kunstgeschichte,* VI, 1937, 218–38.

————, Review: *Pittura italiana del duecento e trecento, catalogo della mostra giottesca,* in *Zeitschrift für Kunstgeschichte,* XII, 1949, 125–29.

Offner, R., "Two Unknown Paintings by Taddeo Gaddi," in *Studies in Florentine Painting, the Fourteenth Century,* New York, 1927.

————, "Giotto, Non-Giotto," *Burlington Magazine,* LXXIV, 1939, 259–68; LXXV, 1939, 96–113.

————, *A Critical and Historical Corpus of Florentine Painting,* 16 vols., New York, 1930–81 (sec. III, vols. 3–6 with K. Steinweg; *Supplement: A Legacy of Attributions. The Fourteenth Century,* 1981, ed. H. Maginnis).

Paccagnini, G., *Simone Martini,* Milan, 1957 (Italian edition, 1955).

————, in *Encyclopedia of World Art,* IX, New York, 1964, cols. 502 and 506.

Pallucchini, P., *La pittura veneziana del trecento,* Venice, 1964.

Palumbo, G., ed., *Giotto e i giotteschi in Assisi,* Rome, 1969. See also M. Gosebruch, G. Marchini, V. Mariani, G. Previtali, and C. Volpe.

Parronchi, A., "Attivita del 'Maestro di Santa Cecilia,'" *Rivista d'arte,* XXI, 1939, 193–228.

Petrarch, F., *Le familiari, libri I–IV,* ed. U. Dotti, Urbino, 1970, 482–501.

Petrarch, P., *Testamentum*—see Mommsen.

Perdrizet, P., *La Vierge de Miséricorde; étude d'un thème iconographique,* Paris, 1908.

Previtali, G., "Le cappelle di San Nicola e di S. Maria Maddalena nella chiesa inferiore di San Francesco," in *Giotto e i giotteschi in Assisi,* ed. G. Palumbo, Rome, 1969, 93–130.

————, *Giotto e la sua bottega,* Milan, 1967; 2nd ed., Milan, 1974.

Procacci, U., "Relazione di lavori eseguiti agli affreschi di Giotto nelle cappelle Bardi e Peruzzi in S. Croce," *Rivista d'arte,* XIX, 1937, 377–89.

Rambaldi, P. L., "Postilla al passo di Riccobaldo," *Rivista d'arte,* XIX, 1937, 349–56.

Rimini, *Mostra della pittura riminese del trecento, catalogo,* ed. C. Brandi, Rimini, 1935.

Rintelen, F., *Giotto und die Giotto-Apokryphen,* Leipzig, Munich, 1912; 2nd ed., Basel, 1923.

Rosenthal, E., *Giotto in der mittelalterlichen Geistesentwicklung,* Augsburg, 1924.

Rowland, B., Jr., "A Fresco Cycle from Spoleto," *Art in America,* XIX, 1931, 224–30.

Ruf, P. Gerhard, *S. Francesco e S. Bonaventura, un interpetazione storico-salvifica degli affreschi della* navata nella chiesa superiore di San Francesco in Assisi alla luce della teologia di San Bonaventura, Assisi, 1974.

Rusconi, A. J., *Assisi,* Bergamo (n.d.) [Italia artistica, no. 89].

Sabatier, P., *Le Speculum Perfectionis; ou, Mémoires de frère Léon,* Manchester, 1928 [British Society of Franciscan Studies, XIII].

————, ed., *Actus beati Francisci et sociorum eius,* in *Collection d'études et de documents sur l'histoire religieuse et littéraire du moyen-âge,* IV, 1902.

Schlosser, J., *Lorenzo Ghibertis Denkwürdigkeiten,* Berlin, 1912.

————, "Giusto's Fresken in Padua und die Vorlaufer der Stanza della Segnatura," *Jahrbuch der kunsthistorischen Sammlungen des Allerhöchsten Kaiserhauses,* XVII, 1896, 13–100, esp. 44–52.

Schmarsow, A., *Kompositionsgesetze der Franziskuslegende in der Oberkirche zu Assisi,* Leipzig, 1919.

Schrade, H., *Franz von Assisi und Giotto,* Cologne, 1964.

Schubring, P., Review: G. Vitzthum, *Bernardo Daddi,* in *Kunstchronik,* n.s., XV, 1904, 545–46.

Schuchert, A., *S. Maria Maggiore zu Rom. Die Grundungsgeschichte der Basilika und die ursprüngliche Apsisanlage,* Vatican City, 1939.

Simon, R., Review: H. Belting, *Die Oberkirche von San Francesco in Assisi,* in *Burlington Magazine,* CXXIII, 1981, 44–46.

————, "Towards a Relative Chronology of the Frescoes in the Lower Church of St. Francis at Assisi," *Burlington Magazine,* CXVIII, 1976, 361–66.

Sinibaldi, G., *I Lorenzetti,* Siena, 1933.

Sirén, O., *Giotto and Some of His Followers,* Cambridge (Mass.), London, and Oxford, 1917.

Smart, A., "The St. Cecilia Master and His School at Assisi," *Burlington Magazine,* CII, 1960, 405–13, 430–37.

————, *The Assisi Problem and the Art of Giotto,* Oxford, 1971.

————, "The *Speculum Perfectionis* and Bellini's Frick St. Francis," *Apollo,* XCVII, 1973, 470–76.

Steinweg, K., "Due pannelli sconosciuti degli armadi di S. Croce di Taddeo Gaddi," *Rivista d'arte,* XIX, 1937, 36–44.

Stubblebine, J., *Guido da Siena,* Princeton, 1964.

————, *Duccio di Buoninsegna and His School,* 2 vols., Princeton, 1979.

————, "An Altarpiece by Giuliano da Rimini," *Fenway Court* (Gardner Museum publication), 1982, 14–27.

Suida, W., "Einige florentinische Maler aus der Zeit des Übergangs vom Duecento ins Trecento," *Jahrbuch des preussischen Kunstsammlungen,* XXVI, 1905, 89–106.

Supino, I. B., *La basilica di San Francesco d'Assisi,* Bologna, 1924.

————, "La cappella di Gian Gaetano Orsini nella basilica di San Francesco," *Bollettino d'arte,* VI, 1926–27, 131–35.

————, *Giotto,* 2 vols., Florence, 1920.

Sussmann, V., "Maria mit dem Schutzmantel," *Marburger Jahrbuch für Kunstwissenschaft,* V, 1929, 285–351.

Tatham, E. R., *Francesco Petrarca, the First Modern Man of Letters; His Life and Correspondence (1304–1347),* 2 vols., London, 1925–26.

Tintori, L., "Il bianco di piombo nelle pitture murali della basilica di San Francesco ad Assisi," *Studies in Late Medieval and Renaissance Painting in Honor of Millard Meiss,* New York, 1977, 437–44.

————, and M. Meiss, *The Paintings of the Life of St. Francis in Assisi,* New York, 1962.

Toesca, I., *Andrea e Nino Pisano,* Florence, 1950.

Toesca, P., *Gli affreschi della vita di S. Francesco nella chiesa superiore del santuario di Assisi,* 2 vols., Florence, 1946(?) [Artis Monumenta photographice edita, III].

————, *Gli affreschi del Vecchio e del Nuovo Testamento nella chiesa superiore del Santuario di Assisi,* 3 vols., Florence, 1948 [Artis Monumenta photographice edita, IV].

————, *Florentine Painting of the Trecento,* Florence [1929].

————, *Giotto,* Turin, 1941 [I grandi italiani, colla di biografie].

————, *Pietro Cavallini,* Milan, 1959.

————, *Storia dell'arte italiana,* I: *Il medioevo,* Turin, 1927; II: *Il Trecento,* Turin, 1951 (reprinted 1971).

Tonini, L., "Di Bitonto e della sua tavola di S. Giuliano non che di alcuni pittori che furono in Rimini," *Atti della deputazione di storia patria per la provincia di Romagna,* II, 1864, 1–9.

Trachtenberg, M., *The Campanile of Florence Cathedral. Giotto's Tower,* New York, 1971.

Vasari, G., *Le vite de' più eccellenti pittori, scultori ed architettori, scritte da Giorgio Vasari pittore aretino,* 9 vols., ed. G. Milanesi, Florence, 1878–85.

———, *Le vite de' più eccellenti pittori, scultori e architettori nella redazione del 1550 e 1568,* eds. R. Bettarini and P. Barocchi, 3 vols., Florence, 1966–71.

Venturi, A., *Storia dell'arte italiana,* 11 vols. in 27, Milan, 1901–40.

Volpe, C., "La formazione di Giotto nella cultura di Assisi," in *Giotto e i giotteschi,* ed. G. Palumbo, Rome, 1969, 15–59.

———, *La pittura riminese del trecento,* Milan, 1965.

———, "Preistoria di Duccio," *Paragone,* no. 49, 1954, 4–22.

Wadding, L., *Annales minorum seu trium ordinum a S. Francisco institutorum,* II, Rome, 1732, 397.

Waetzoldt, S., *Die Kopien des 17. Jahrhunderts nach Mosaiken und Wandmalerei in Rom* [Romische Forschungen der Bibliotheca Hertziana, no. 18], Vienna and Munich, 1964.

Wakefield, D., *Stendhal and the Arts,* New York and London, 1973.

Walsh, B., "A Note on Giotto's 'Vision of Brother Agostino and the Bishop of Assisi,' Bardi Chapel," *Art Bulletin,* LXII, 1980, 20–23.

White, J., *Art and Architecture in Italy, 1250 to 1400,* Baltimore, 1966.

———, *The Birth and Rebirth of Pictorial Space,* London, 1957; 2nd ed., London and Boston, 1967.

———, "Cavallini and the Lost Frescoes in S. Paolo," *Journal of the Warburg and Courtauld Institutes,* XIX, 1956, 84–95.

———, "Cimabue and Assisi: Working Methods and Art Historical Consequences," *Art History,* IV, no. 4, 1981, 372–73.

———, "Giotto's Use of Architecture in 'The Expulsion of Joachim' and 'The Entry into Jerusalem' at Padua," *Burlington Magazine,* CXV, 1973, 439–47.

———, "The Date of the 'St. Francis Legend' at Assisi," *Burlington Magazine,* XCVIII, 1956, 344–51.

Witte, K., "Der Sacro Convento in Assisi," *Kunstblatt,* 1821, no. 40, 163; no. 42, 166–67; no. 44, 175–76; no. 45, 178–80; no. 46, 180–84.

Zeri, F., "Una 'Deposizione' di scuola riminese," *Paragone,* no. 99, 1958, 47–54.

Zocca, E., *Assisi, catalogo delle cose d'arte e d'antichità,* Rome, 1936.

Index